DEVLIN CULLIVER

{An-tee-tuh-m}

Signing

Day

DEVLIN CULLIVER

An Antietam Jones Mystery

Trient Press
3375 S Rainbow Blvd
#81710, SMB 13135
Las Vegas,NV 89180

Ordering Information:
Quantity sales. Special discounts are available on quantity purchases by corporations, associations, and others. For details, contact the publisher at the address above.
Orders by U.S. trade bookstores and wholesalers. Please contact Trient Press: Tel: (775) 996-3844; or visit www.trientpress.com.

Printed in the United States of America

Publisher's Cataloging-in-Publication data
CULLIVER, DEVLIN
A title of a book : Signing Day

ISBN

Hard Cover	978-1-953975-90-4
Paperback	978-1-953975-91-1
E-book	978-1-953975-92-8

An
Antietam Jones
Mystery

Dedicated to the South High Warriors

Garcia Lane, Ellis Sullivan Scott Ivy, Tyrone Ivy, Willie Green, Teddy Owens, T-Lee Chism, Tommy Harris, Delbert Tillery, Tamron Smith, Kenny Boone, Mark Stanford, Kendall Cage, Ronald Page, Keith Page, Greg Brown, Brian, Dwayne & Raymond Marrow, Keith Saunders, Louis Gilbert, Tony Tellington, Gary & Kent Thornton, Ivan Williams, Leon Williams, Keith Lawrence, LJ Williams, David Robinson, John McWilson, Willie Green, Kevin Berkley, Sam Burns, Toni Jack, J.J. Jackson, Bobby Washington, Scott Washington, Tony Jones, Keith Posey, Terry Chatman, Terry Pearson, Tony Harris, Coach Roland Smith, Marlon McGaughy, Haryl and Daryl Dabney, Kevin Davis, George "Rat" Thomas, Kevin Williams, Jerry Fordham, Randy Cooper, Stanley Cooper, David Clinckscale, David Robinson, Kevin Gilbert, Blue Gilbert, Brian "Drac" Ford, Mike Cotton, Willie Briskey, Glenn Williams, Corey Spragling, Walter Jones, Chris Williams, Victor Bush, The Rushtons, Charles Ruffin, Steve Bailey, Rod King, King-Lo, Jody McCulloh, Randy Nuby, Harry Arroyo, Marvin Moses, Marvin Oates, Mark and Keith Mitchell, Alonzo Bailey, Tim Beechum, Jay Cunningham.

The City: Donnie Harris, Tim McWilson, Wendell Stewart, Chris Amil, Ramone Amil, Andre Jackson, Tyrone Ware, Floyd Showers, David R. Culliver, David G. Culliver, Daniel Culliver, Asim Pleas, Kevin Harris, Ron Lewis, Herman Hill, Roy "Stretch" Donaldson, David Wilkins, Todd Finley, Mike Ivey, Kevin Madison, Terry Williams, Greg Richardson, Jeff Lampkin, Scott Dudley, Tim Parker, Terica Jones, Jeremy Bachelor, Raymond Allen, Danny Allen, Walter "T" Madison, Eddie Blockson, Collin and Zerrick Staples, Tony and Kenny

Donaldson, Tanya Donaldson, Eric EB Berry, Mark McClendon, D. Pixley, Brother Penson, J.C. Penny, Tony Lynch, Shaun Lane, Tim Rutledge, John “Stoney” Toomer, my dude Lloyd “Salt” Hopkins, Steve Johnson, Sterling Hayden, Oslo Taylor, Rick Baskins, Mark Shaw, Jamie Fortune, Kelly Fortune, Vince Marrow, Allen Coleman, Juice Coleman, Eryek Griffin, John Grizzard, Allen Jones, Mike Clarett, Ted Bell, Maurice Clarett, Dave Dawson, Mike Flores, Derrick Lewis, Eddie Thomas, Duane Thomas, Steven Clinkscale, Trevor Starghill, Jamie Austin, Anthony Poole, Leo Hawkins, Brad Smith, Anthony Floyd, Keilen Dykes, Braylon Heard, Derrick Morgan, Freddie and Mark Spain, Blaine Griffin, Lance Jones, John Greene, Wilson Humphrey, Shane Johnson, Dawn Powell. Angela & Cyrstal Turnage. Jada Ransome, Lateefa Shakoor, Tim Caffey, Deollo Anderson, Travis Jones, Harry Johnson, Sterling Hayden, Robert Nall, Clinton Lynch, Alonzo Ransome, Kevin Ellerbee, Corey Phillips, Brad Smith, Booker Newberry Jr., Terry Williams, Kenny Coleman, Terry Taylor, Jamie Mendez, Terrance Phillips.

Forever grateful to my Hagstrom House Braves Coaches for having the most profound influence in my life: Head Coach Leroy Williams, Coach Roy Donaldson, Coach Hugh Campbell, Coach Clarence Anderson, Coach Andy Lane, Coach Thomas Harris, Coach Stick, Coach Richard Williams, Coach Lucius, Coach Richard Blacksheer & Coach Al Jones.

Thanks to My family: My mother and Father, my Grandparents, my brothers David, Daniel, Lamar, and Chuckie, my sister Tiffany, my cousins Binky & Monica, Tanya, Renee, Pixie Mrs. Harris, Kira & Crystal, Mr. & Mrs. Barnes.

Thanks to the crew: Chuckie, T-Lee, Tommy, Reece, Wendell, Arnette, Roy, Anthony, Stacy, Daryl & Tim.

To my Northside family: Coach, Tony, Kenny, Stretch, Tanya, Terrance, Corey, Tony L & Floyd

To the CORE

To five of the Six Indestructible Souls: Marwin, John, Marzell, Darby & C1
Special Thanks to: Coach Congemi, Andrew L. Greer & Sam Nestor

Dedicated to-

Thomas "Doc" Smith, for the love of one man to boy.

Mr. Roosevelt Harris, for always being an extension of my family tree.

Head Coach Leroy Williams, for teaching me leadership, love and style.

Coach Roy Donaldson for creating me into a tough kid-one that you would support a lifetime.

Coach Clarence Anderson, for developing my football IQ at a young age, for the chips, sodas and the rides home…and for that night when the world ended.

Robert Bell, for having a vision that included me inside of it.

&

Mark McClendon, the first person to tell me I was good!

For Marzell Pink & De'Van Bogard…man!!!!

I'm going home
Back to the place where I belong
And where your love has always been enough for me
I'm not running from
No, I think you got me all wrong
I don't regret this life I chose for me
But these places and these faces are getting old
So I'm going home
Well, I'm going home

-Daughtry

Introduction

How Antietam Anthony Jones Was Born

By Devlin Culliver

I am not so conceited as to conceive that it is possible for me to account completely for my own book, *signing day.* Nevertheless, I am going to try to be as accountable for as much of it as I can-the characters in it, the material that went into it, and my own years of being a high school football coach and a fisher of young men that has influenced the material of which I wrote about.

In an imaginative novel like this, a few important things blend-together; my growing up as a black male in an America and trying to help and raise black males in America. In this novel, several lives merge in a small urban city and high school. Many of the characters are fictional but some are people that had an influence on me as I wrote many of the words of this book. The indirect mention of certain men that are in the book, men like Garcia Lane and Pastor Kenny Donaldson are real people and were a great part of my growing up in the city of Youngstown, Ohio.

Youngstown is a hard place. A hard enough of a place that we had to refine our athletic skills on empty-partially grassed lots, cracked concrete playgrounds, some on the street corners, and some in dark back alleyways and many on the basketball courts and football fields. None of us unspoiled, none of us polished or smooth, just little black boys in search of our manhood-through games.

The more that I wrote, the more I thought about why I was writing, the more I came to regard my own imagination as a kind of self-generating adhesive which was able to glue facts, history and fiction into a cloudy day type of mystery crime novel. As my pens ink sank into the paper, Antietam grew into a superhero, but not one without flaws and fears, or the abilities to make bad decisions or mistakes. He does not possess any mystical or mutant powers that will allow him to fly or create magic spells to defeat the bad-guys or monstrous dragons, but he is ingratiated with the power of the human spirit. Antietam Jones is kindhearted, plain and simple but possess a hard edge personality when he needs it. He is a Blackman who has dedicated his life to helping young men, much like I have in this present day all along with all my mistakes and hurts that I have caused people along the way-mostly unintentional if being honest.

Antietam has to survive much like a dog chained up in a backyard. A dog that can see his freedom through the diamond patterns of the fence or through the gaps in the bushes that block his clear view, but steadily-rhythmically treads that same path of dirt in HOPES that that chain will someday break or his captor releases him.

He becomes a go-to-guy of sorts, he is willing to be that person to every boy he encounters, but only because of his love and inner obligation to repay all the men who have brought him up to this moment of his life.

He walks through the novel trying to find all that eludes him. His name, rooted in the slaves of the Civil War. His grit, from the gravediggers that sat along the banks of sunken road tasked with gathering up the dead white boys whose bodies overlapped the grass.

That part of his life he knew about but there were traces of broken tracks that he wanted and needed to piece together.

The personality he inherited, from his distant-distant-distant cousin, the black spy for the Pinkerton Detective Agency, W. H. Ringgold, a free man who had been forced to work on a Virginia riverboat that was moving Confederate troops and supplies. Ringgold purposely overheard Confederate plans. Ringgold told Pinkerton all he knew about Confederate fortifications on the Virginia peninsula and when General George B. McClellan began his peninsula campaign in March 1862, the best intelligence he had was from Ringgold. The Black Pinkerton Detectives of the 1850's was infused in his DNA and fueled his curiosity to find answers.

He comes upon characters much like in the comic books and movies, each of them serving an important part of a search for things that were already there right in front of them. Characters like Head Football Coach and Principal-Big Browbow, Marva Browbow, Hutch

'Hue" Campbell, Isum Duart and many more. All of them playing a significant role and function in the story but none more important than Antietam himself-he is the star of the story even without really trying to be.

During my younger years as a fine artist, I deliberately styled my art after the work of Charles White and Ernie Barnes and my brush created on canvas original works that reflected their styles encompassed in my own uniqueness. The birth of Antietam Anthony Jones came out of those years as a painter.

In my childhood I saw everything as a canvas and a story that I could tell with pencils, brushes and paint in an attempt to create the things my young eyes laid witness too each day. I sketched and painted whenever I was not running up and down the block playing football with my neighborhood friends.

Art and football ignited my spirit and has carried me throughout my life both holding equal importance. Every day I was running, every day I was drawing, every day I was growing in body and spirit. The older I got the better at football I became, the older I got the better artist I became. I used one to manifest the other. Football gave me the opportunity to get formally trained at a university art school.

It was not until my adulthood and flying off the branch of the tree my parents grew for me, that I thought to seriously write a novel about Antietam, so my entire life I had been crafting him in my mind, sort of living out his life and then putting that life first on canvas and then on paper. I began writing his story fifteen years ago after bad memories of having a mental breakdown of being a victim of a drive-by shooting and my destroyed relationship with my father in 1991.

The name Antietam, pronounced [an-tee-tuh-m] originally was Derrick then changed to Hopeful, he, or it, would be safe to say *(I)* was hopeful that one day a father and son could mend what was broken between them, hopeful that the recollections of those bullets that almost killed me would someday disappear. Antietam, that name and the thoughts that I kept under lock and key my whole life began to pour out onto paper. As I said, I had already painted Hopeful Jones and his life several times but now I wanted to write about him. Over the course of these last 15 years, I have completed chapters, ripped them up, deleted them, and started again but now he is here for you to meet and get to know.

In the novel Antietam learns from his uncle. He learns the lessons of life being raised by a man and having no influence of a woman around the house. That didn't matter. One may think that that would present a problem or deficiency in his manliness but on the contrary, he becomes a man with all the nurturing and love that a man is supposed to have inside himself. He learned what true appreciation was by having a man like his uncle serve as his father and his first teacher. That appreciation, his uncle learned in Vietnam when one of his Army friends gave him a fresh pair of socks, which you will learn of "what that means" when you get to that part of the novel. The appreciation, of only having scraps to eat because there was nothing else when times were tough. So when the two of them struggled, the young Antietam never complained because he had that appreciation instilled within him. That is the example shown in this book, Antietam's Godly truth comes out when he need's it most, his gratefulness for his life.

I tried to make Antietam pour verbal milk into a metaphorical cup for the readers to drink. He has the ability to use vocabulary that is complex yet simple and relaxed enough to put the reader at ease. He has mastered that difficult task that most educated black people have to master, the task of being able to speak what America considers intelligent (white) to have a good job and that "street slang" to survive in the so-called inner cities of this country.

I love Antietam. I love everything about him from his feet to his head. I spent years creating him through the fabric of America, first as a single thread that turned into a blanket that was wide enough to cover every ghetto in this country. I love the man he grows to become. I love the mistakes and fears that he lives with each day.

Through the words on a page or computer screen, iPhone or tablet, I protect him from the evil ones, from the devil, from anyone or anything that tries to erase him from existing. I have to care about him the same way I care about myself. So for Antietam Jones I fight for him and with him back to back versus all comers. Speaking of that old devil called Satan, he shows up from time to time to cause his havoc and confusion.

The stories I write are like jam in a mason jar, jam that I spread on the wheat bread-the people. The characters that I create come to life through fiction because without fiction we don't exist. We learn about who we are not so much from our parents or grandparents but more through made up tales about where we have been and where we can go. Fiction gave the world a look into our lives through print. Think about that for a second. Think about Walter Younger in the book "A Raisin in the Sun." Walter Younger represented Black men and the struggles we face each day of our lives and so how else would the world know about us if Lorraine Hansberry had not written it down.

The Marvel Character Luke Cage is a real person to me, he became "real" through fiction. The way he was described, his powers, his street slang, the neighborhood he came from, all of that was my life in reality.

So-when you read about all the characters that I write about in m my novels, their creative names and nicknames, let them soak into your soul and know, that they are real too.

As you read each word, through each chapter, a story will unfold-a shocking sorta-true fictional story that not only causes Antietam to change but also each character around him as well. This novel is about the search for the truth, the truth on the streets, in a locker room and the truth of God. Be sure to pay attention to the words infused in this novel. Words left behind for us and only us…the truth.

"Have You Ever Seen The Rain"

Someone told me long ago
There's a calm before the storm
I know, it's been coming for some time
When it's over, so they say
It'll rain a sunny day
I know, shining down like water

I wanna know, have you ever seen the rain?
I wanna know, have you ever seen the rain?
Coming down on a sunny day

Yesterday, and days before
Sun is cold and rain is hard
I know, been that way for all my time
'Til forever, on it goes
Through the circle, fast and slow
I know, it can't stop, I wonder

I wanna know, have you ever seen the rain?
I wanna know, have you ever seen the rain?
Coming down on a sunny day

Yeah!

I wanna know, have you ever seen the rain?
I wanna know, have you ever seen the rain?
Coming down on a sunny day

-Creedence Clearwater Revival

Pre-game

Awk-a-bawk

IT WAS 1981 at the height of the Atlanta child murders.

Our teacher Mrs. Walton told us to stop talking. I got quiet as fast as I could because she had already called home a few weeks ago because she said that I kept talking after she asked me three times to stop. She lied though-it was only two times. I sat up square in my seat hoping that she would see that I was a changed man after the whooping my uncle gave me for getting that phone call.

"Attention everyone," she yelled out.

The class settled down except for a few knuckleheads in the back who turned their voices into soft whispers but still talked the whole time. Lovely turned around and told them to shut-up. Lovely Banks was the girl everybody in the class was afraid of. She wasn't lovely at all, at least to me she wasn't, not sure why her mamma named her that. Her face alone was ugly enough to scare you into listening to her, when she caught an attitude, even the nastiest dog, trained or stray better step aside.

"Excuse me Lovely, I don't need your help," our teacher told her.

Lovely's lips twisted up like she was sucking on a lemon and popped them. She slouched down in the chair and waited for more from the teacher.

"Now-listen up, the Annual Paper Airplane contest is this Friday downtown at the Market Street Bridge. It is the 60th year celebration. I am passing out a field trip permission slip and the rules for the contest. I am also handing out instructions on how-to-make paper airplanes if you already don't know how. There are three grades eligible to enter, third, fourth and fifth. Along with the judged categories of airplane construction, flight and decoration. On the entry form which is also coming around, you can pick which category you want to enter but the most you can chose is two. Please take all the forms home and get them signed and bring them back before Friday…are there any questions before we get back to the lesson."

"Do we have to make a plane?" Carlton asked Mrs. Walton.

"No… but you have to get the field trip form signed by your parent or you will spending your school day in a split class with the fifth graders."

I considered myself a master paper airplane maker. I missed last year's contest because that was the day I broke my arm falling down the cellar steps going to get my shirt out the dryer. I fell because I walked into a spider web. Me and my uncle spent the whole day at the hospital, so I missed the contest. I made up in my head that nothing would stop me from signing up and winning this year.

Making airplanes was easy for me. I had stolen a how-to-book from the school library when I was in second grade and had it ever since. I was excited for the rest of the day and would start making my test planes once I got home from football practice.

The last five minutes of each day the principal, Mr. Greggs comes on the P-A system to make the last announcements before we go home. Mr. Greggs was mean but a fair type of dude. He was bald at the top but kept the hair on the outside on his head. He seem not to know that a black man shouldn't wear his hair that way around a bunch of rude ass black kids. We used to laugh at that every time we saw him. He dressed pretty nice and was a pretty good principal, better than the last one we had that got caught drunk coming out of a bar one night. He got fired.

"Good afternoon Princeton Elementary School students and staff. This is your Principal Mr. Greggs…I need your attention and total silence…teachers please make sure your classes are quiet…I wanted to caution every student walking home to make sure you are going straight home…do not, and I repeat do not stop and talk to anyone that you do not know. I am not sure if any of you have been watching the news and I am not telling you this to alarm or scare you... however you need to be aware that it has been reported that there have been children missing in the city of Atlanta, Georgia, black children...even though Atlanta is many-many miles away from Ohio, we must take every precaution possible to ensure your safety. So in saying that, please walk home in groups or get a ride with someone... again this is not to scare you but this information has to be shared. Lastly, I need all teachers outside when the bell rings...thank you."

I was frozen, letting what he said push aside all my thoughts of making that paper airplane after football practice. School let out just and it started to rain. I went to my locker, grabbed my things and headed to Idora Field where we practiced at. It was only a few blocks from the school.

Practice lasted an hour and was more fun than usual because today we got muddy. We finished out last sprint and Coach Greer gathered us up and we took a knee. I knew that somewhere in his after-practice speech, he would mention the stuff about what the Principal told us in school.

"Eyes-up," he said.

We all looked up into his face. He was one of us-that is what he would always say to remind us that he once came from a place like this one. He told us that his mother moved him from California to Ohio when he was a boy. So he grew up around here but on the upper Eastside. We all liked coach, he was cool.

"Good practice today. Let's come back tomorrow and get better. Let's make sure we are getting all our school work done... and I need you guys to go straight home. I don't want to see any of yall hanging around, as soon as I dismiss you go home, don't stop nowhere for no reason. Go home and watch the news and learn about some of the things that are going on in this country. We all heard about what is going on in Atlanta, don't be afraid, just be cautions and aware. That is why I am telling you to go straight home."

My head dropped. I was staring at the wet grass thinking about the words coach just said. I was afraid this time, when I wasn't before when I heard the same thing from the principal.

"Understood?" Coach yelled.

"Yes Coach," we said.

He dismissed us. Donnie and Andrew both looked at me. Andrew lived around the corner from me and Donnie a few streets from him. We started walking home. It was quiet for a long while as we walked in the rain, through puddle after puddle toward the bridge that we had to cross every day. Even though we crossed that bridge day after day since were little, this time it felt different. Like someone was watching us from below. I wanted to say something but I just didn't know what, so I just thought about the contest as we came to the other side.

We walked Andrew to his front steps, something we never did in the past. Usually when we hit his corner he would head off on his own, but today, for some reason our feet led right up to his door.

"Later man," I said.

"Later," he said back.

He looked back at us as if we would never see him again and right before he went in the door he said, "its' Awk-a-bawk aint it?"

"Man he ain't real, that's just some talk," Donnie said fast.

We left without saying anymore.

Awk-a-bawk was a killer of kids. He lived in the Dewey-Woods under the bridge. They said he was 100 years old-still big and strong and could never be caught or killed. His teeth were sharp like a nails and his eyes were all black like the coal that the men shovel at the steel mill. His wore bummy clothes that were torn and ripped and he smelled like piss. His shoes were busted and his feet had dried blood on them. They said he lived in the farthest part of the woods in a small house that he built and if he catches you, then you can never get away and you will disappear never to be found again.

I knew that Donnie was running those same thoughts in his head because we had always heard about the man under the Dewey Street Bridge named Awk-a-bawk.

***

It was 1981 at the height of the Atlanta child murders.

I laid in my bed past twelve o'clock thinking about what Andrew had asked us today. I wasn't a scary type of dude. I watched scary movies on TV all the time but this was real. I prayed not to be afraid tomorrow. I prayed for Andrew and Donnie. I laid there for a few more minutes thinking about when I first heard about him. Second grade, Tommy Reyes, on Halloween, he said his older brother Danny told him about the man under the bridge. By the time school was that day, we all knew about Awk-a-bawk.

The next day at recess we were flying our practice planes making sure the different folds and creases would work once we let them fly from our hands. My plane always soared higher and longer than my classmates. I took this serious, folding, creasing, pressing and then fluffing the wings of my plane. I don't like much, but what I did like was always based around, football-reading-drawing and making paper airplanes. I didn't want to be a pilot or nothing like that, I guess it's just the-making part it is what I really like.

A kid named Jerome in my class who messed with all of us all the time. Not like a bully but more like a pest-type of dude, you know always trying to get you to slap box with him or crack some jokes. He was a cool dude other than the fact that he smelled musty or funky as the girls called it and that was the one thing that everybody hated about him. For some reason his smell and his clowning around didn't bother me, but Andrew hated his guts and Donnie ignored him.

We flew our planes from one end of the parking lot to the next. Andrew's plane landed right at the tip of Jerome's' rusty sneakers. Instead of picking it up and flying it back, he stepped on it and ran off laughing.

Andrew ran after him and grabbed the back of his collar and yanked him to the ground. The recess monitor, Mrs. Sinkovich yelled to stop but Andrew was already in mid-punch by that point. I ran over and pulled Drew back trying to calm him down. He was so mad that tears came down his face.

The bell rang and we walked back into the school, Andrew's chest still going up and down and his fist were still balled up until the principal came and got him and Jerome. They both came back to class and Andrew was no longer mad but Jerome was holding a tissue on his lip from the punch. They both sat down and started their classwork.

Most of the time around here, if a fight breaks out during school, it always happens again after-school. I made sure Andrew didn't have a second round with Jerome. As soon as the last bell rang we hurried and got out the back door away from the crowd that was waiting in the front to witness round-two.

***

Tuesday was cloudy, but no rain was coming down, my practice pants and jersey was still wet from yesterday and that's not a good feeling…being soggy. Living in a valley on a cloudy day sometimes after a rain fog comes up from under the bridge, or maybe it comes down from the sky. Practice was over and we headed on our way and through the fog, right before we got to the first sidewalk cement block of the bridge, we could see police lights and a big red ambulance parked sideways in the street. Around here when you see that, it usually means a dead body that they don't want you to see.

There was a black cop waving people back from trying to get a closer look at what was going on. He pushed us back up the sidewalk away from the edge of the bridge. Andrew and Donnie looked at me. I looked at them. We didn't speak or make any sounds. Everything was in slow motion around us. That's when it happened.

Three cops struggled as they pulled a body up the steep side of the hill on the side of the bridge. It was a boy covered in mud and leaves, he had scratches all over his face and arms. His eyes seemed to be coming out of his head in fear of whatever it was he had seen before he died. Maybe it was Awk-a-bawk that killed him I thought to myself.

Donnie grabbed the sleeve of my coat and I reached out and pulled Andrew close to me. P walked in tight behind Andrew. I knew we all had the same thought and picture in our heads. Awk-a-bawk! Even though we had never seen him we had heard enough stories and descriptions to see him in our minds. Donnie's grip got tighter on my sleeve.

I backed us all up and we turned around and ran away from that place. We ran until we couldn't run anymore. We cut down Idlewood Street and through Falls Playground until we were on our street. We walked Andrew up to his door again. This time he didn't look back at us, he just went inside.

Donnie dapped me up and took off. Now I was alone and this was really the first time I felt it in my soul. I walked down to the sidewalk as fast as I could holding back the fear that was making me want to jog, by the time I got to my house the news had spread about what we had seen with our own eyes.

It was seven o'clock and I sat close to my uncle and watched the news. The first story reported was about that boy. His name was Kenny Parker from Cohasset Street. He was my age. He went to Calvary Prep Academy a few blocks from our school. The man on the news said that the boy appeared to be strangled and was left under the bridge. Someone made an anonymous call to the police about there being a dead boy under the bridge. The reporter said his shoes were off when he was found and that is what stuck with me the most. A kid down in the bushes on a foggy day alone…with no shoes on.

So Ima end this lecture and I betcha, those who kick dirt and do time I'm gonna get cha, cause I be kicking the real, while they be losing the race trying to chase mass appeal.

-Gang Starr

1

1985 MASS APPEAL

WE ADMIRED A local drug dealer named Robert Bell, my friend Donnie and me. Don't jump to any conclusions Robert Bell was one of the best men I had ever met up to that point in my life. I know the contradiction of being a drug dealer and a good guy don't match up but I can't explain it any other way, and if I tried to explain it or break it down, I would say this, that outwardly bad actions don't always reveal a man's true goodness within his heart.

Like most kids in *ain't got cities*, our actions revolved around sports, Saturday cartoons and penny candy, but what we were the most impressed by were muscle cars-hot rods, the fancy, brightly painted, rimmed-out kind. The kind Robert Bell drove.

The streets in the summer of Youngstown were like a box of Mike & Ike's, candy coated treats with wheels for our eyes to eat up rolling down every block of our neighborhood.

The color turquoise is a beautiful color. The first time I saw it was in school when Crayola came out with the 64 pack of crayons. Robert drove a 1965 customized, turquoise glazed, drop-top Pontiac GTO.

On my street, no one drove a car like that those cars with odd colored glossy paint jobs, with six-inch white wall tires, wrapped around twenty-four inch rims. The cars on my block were modest in color and style-regular-people's rides.

***

Robert ran with a Puerto Rican dude named Jayo Ramos. Together they controlled the Southside drug game and other than the local high school football players, those were the two role models that got lifted up for us to look at in our neighborhood.

I was blessed you could say, because I lived with my uncle Thomas Smith, his friends called him Kay-Kee and I had enough fear of him to never let the thought of selling drugs cross my mind or let a dude like Robert Bell move into his spot as my main role model. Donnie had his mother who had the same rule.

Still, we both thought Robert was an interesting enough character and had some things two kids like us could dig.

He was a good athlete but never played any organized sports. Word was he would try out for football, basketball and track every year and was good enough to play all three, but according to the streets, his personality couldn't stand the structure of being coached.

He graduated from Southside High School in 1977 and immediately got caught up in the drug culture and he became an expert at the game of the streets, hustling, running-cons and moving dope and money in and out of pockets of wannabe drug chiefs and dope fiends.

He dressed nice. He always had the latest sneakers on his feet and top name brand jeans and shirts. He rocked two-piece sweat outfits on the regular. He had a clothes booster that would drop off the hottest most popular apparel.

He was what my cousin called a "neighborhood guy" meaning that he was one of us, or one of ours.

Robert and Jayo were the heads of a small cartel-The Costilano. Under them, was a mixed-boy, Billy (B-Money), he was good at adding up numbers. His mother was white and his father was a successful construction company owner, the only black owned business in town. B-Money handled all the dollars and made sure that everything they did flowed downstream and never upstream which is where the Feds camped. Billy was the half-breed boy who grew up in the suburbs but hung out in the hood. He was good at pretending he really wanted to be 100% black.

Under Billy were the expendables: the homies, the security, the young dedicated dudes who stood at the end of dark alleys flashing in and out like rats running from trash can to trash can, the street corner product pushers, feeding the open hands of the fiends and junkies, summer, winter and fall.

Despite it being the dope game, there was a sophistication to it, a pyramid of top and bottom boys and in the middle lived the external providers the ones we never saw face-to-face. They were the lawyers, cops and politicians that were invisible within the walls of the inner bowels of the city. Even though we were young, we knew that those men had to exist somewhere.

***

The frequency of our encounters with Robert came out of something he was good at and that was making money anyway that he could.

He knew that he would have trouble on his hands if my uncle ever caught a whiff of him trying to lead me down the wrong path, but Robert still found a way to get dollars out of me.

He love to race. The streets said that he could have been a tack star if he didn't choose the dope-game, but instead of him using his ability to stride out of the ghetto onto a college campus, he decided to burn rubber showing off the muscle under the hood of GTO or Z28.

Speed, the pumping pistons produced from the cars he designated as *racers* verses the cars he used for *cruising* Hillman Avenue, Hillman Ave-affectionately known as 'the strip.' His cars could harvest six to seven hundred dollars competing vertically on a residential street. He would duel Hillman and the smell of burnt rubber would penetrate our nostrils-as we would watch the white tire smoke ghost the air from one corner to the next.

Speed, the pumping of arms and legs in unison to win a footrace. He was fast like me, like Donnie, and from time to time you could catch him outrunning other grown men who thought they still had enough speed left in their aged legs to out step him.

Robert liked football too; he went to all the games-little league and high school, at first thought, more for the reasons to be-seen, rather than to enjoy a game. It was his red carpet moment. He had an unofficial reserved seat at Southside Stadium, he and Jayo and the all the ladies who fancied their company. The only people that hung in that area were wannabe's or girls who were looking for a status come-up.

He lived three streets down from me on St. Louis Avenue and I would see him almost daily because I was cool with his nephew Maurice, Reece stayed seven houses up from Robert.

I could have walked up my street to the opposite corner, then down to the top end of St. Louis and that route would have kept me from seeing Robert but I never went that way. Something in my psyche wanted to be seen by him, so when me and Donnie would link up, I would purposely walk that way. I liked his attention- Donnie too or maybe, we just liked those girls that hung around him all the time.

It seemed as if right before I passed his house he would appear like a magician from behind a curtain or sometimes he would already be sitting on his porch knowing I was about to come walking around the corner. Each time, he would stop me. At these stops we would talk, laugh and eat.

It was the summer before I entered the 8th grade, when those casual talks turned into business encounters for him.

***

In a neighborhood of no playgrounds, deflated balls with no-net-having basketball hoops that left only left a few choices and that was to make up our own games to play. We played football with old bike tires, baseball with a tennis ball and a broom stick. And when we were really being creative we would jump off garage roofs to see who could land on two feet without falling over, but my main thing was that I loved to run, not just for the sake of running but to see how fast I could make my legs go.

I was the fastest on my street and my reputation quickly spread from block to block. Donnie locked down Ravenwood Ave with his feet. Every street back in those days had a kid who was fast and every now and then, you had to prove it but only if that kid and his friends somehow ended up on your block and was down for a race.

It is one thing being the champion on your block, but another when you take your talent around the corner or across the intersection to the next part of your street where you had to show it and prove it.

There were a bunch of boys around my age, most of them black or Puerto Rican within four to five blocks of where Robert lived; his street was in the middle so it was the place to be in the summer-St. Louis Avenue. Robert was two-plus-two, meaning he was four everybody. He was the neighborhood hero always grilling food, blasting the latest Hip-Hop music out of his car, or popping illegal firecrackers and M-80's on non-fourth of July days.

There were only so many things that kids our age could get into, that could-be-deemed as safe in an unorganized setting. The other shit, would land you in the juvenile detention center or in the basement of a coffin and neither one of those did I want any parts of, so the closest thing to me a being criminal was being near Robert Bell.

Robert was an *opportunist* because he came up with an idea of how to make himself some money that would not involve a pistol or shotgun. He created a "hood track meet" for the neighborhood kids within those five blocks to run against each other. Those friendly racing games that I was coaxed into doing quickly changed. Now he was making me race or should I say us race. We didn't have any other choice least take the chance of being bullied by his team, many who were our age but acted much older and a whole lot tougher.

Robert organized these races as if it was a real business. He had a point spread. One race, no bests-ofves. On the concrete he spray-painted a white line for the start and finish from curb to curb. He had a point man that made sure no one's toe would be over the line.

His drug-dealing associates from all around the city would post up in their fly ass cars with stoutly built women that drove our young eager minds crazy looking at them.

He would pair us by grade or age. I mixed in with kids going to the eighth grade and only a few in the seventh. Donnie paired up with kids going in the seventh-he was a grade behind me.

The matchups didn't really matter to Robert as long as you wasn't a grown ass man, you could get in the race. He would lay money down and took all bets from whoever wanted in and within five minutes, twenty-dollar bills covered the top edges of the curb and the owners of those bills would be standing over their money like tin soldiers.

Robert had a young drudge, a kid called "Fat Toney." Fat Toney was a year younger but he was already hardened from running with Robert and Jayo. He looked older than I did, you could see a dark shadow mustache forming over his lip, when my lip was bald. He was approximately five-six and a solid two-hundred pounds. His face was full like a bulldog and his stomach pushed out tightly through the adult sized shits he wore. He filled out the crispy Levi Jeans, and rocked the white leather Dr. J's, while I had canvas Pro-Keds on my feet.

He wore a gold chain and had an earring in his left ear but all I could concentrate on was that he was fat, and ugly, and even though my uncle had always taught me never to judge a man's looks, with Fat Toney, I couldn't help it. His face was frog in appearance with wide eyes and mouth and no amount of coco-butter lotion could smooth out the rough look of his skin.

I would find myself staring at him, wondering what his parents thought about his clothes his fat face and his involvement with Robert and Jayo or if they even knew, or even cared. Maybe, Fat Toney was like me in that sense, maybe his parents didn't care about him either.

Either way Toney found some love from Robert Bell.

Fat Toney's job was to collect all the money at the end of the race and give it to Billy. Danny would count it up and make sure no one cheated them out on a dollar. Every dollar counted and Toney made sure he picked up every bill. If Robert or Jayo lost, Fat Toney stood still.

The races grew bigger and bigger which made the dollar amounts grow. The more money that hit the curb the bolder Fat Toney became. Here was a kid handling hundreds of dollars and the most my fingers ever touched was a five or ten my uncle would drop me from time to time.

Toney took pride in his job as collector he also took pride in every chance he had to make me feel like I wasn't shit. It was the look of envy and you didn't have to be an adult to know that look. I had never done anything to him for me to deserve the grimace his face delivered me.

Toney and I were lukewarm friends, enough to at least to say 'what-up' to each other. He was from down-the-hill so I would run into him during the vacation months of the year but that's all it ever was to our relationship.

When I showed up, his shoulders would pull back and his voice would get deeper trying to sound older than a seventh grader. His behavior would become loud and brash and when his eyes met mine, his chin would tilt toward the ground and lock in on me without blinking, the coldness of winter over of my relationship with Robert Bell became clear to me. See, even though Robert was making me run, he still treated me nice and showed me love in the form of bragging about me to the crowd. That made Toney feel emotions a kid shouldn't feel at that age. Emotions that make men kill. That evil that was brewing up inside of Fat Toney toward me would prove to be dangerous as the years grew.

I had my first one on one encounter with Fat Toney one day on the side of Robert Bell's house. I had just finished beating a kid in a race, and was drinking water from out of the hose and I guess he wanted some at the same time as I did. I turned the partly rusted faucet and waited for the hopefully cold water to come spilling out into my mouth. I leaned forward and stood stiff legged keeping my sneakers away from the falling water that missed my stuck out tongue. Fat Toney posed eagerly behind me with a stack of money in his hand.

"Hurry up man," he said.

I cut my eyes at him as I kept the flow of water going until I quenched my thirst. He grabbed the hose from my hand as a big gulp shot across my ear and neck. My left foot took a step toward him and my fist automatically balled up preparing for a swing. He smiled, not in friendship and not even in brotherly play, but as if, I were a little boy and he a man. He knew that the world of Robert Bell was only feet away and that he had the upper hand on me. My pride was damaged and I knew that if we fought that I would probably get jumped by the other boys who were not on my side but on Robert Bell's payroll. Part of my mind thought that maybe Robert would side with me and let Fat Toney and me go head to head in a fight, but I wasn't ready to take that chance, so I just walked back to the front of the house, wet eared and neck.

Race after race I learned to ignore Fat Toney and focus on running and winning. The distance was always about six houses long, in football measurement, that is about 75 yards, and that was right down my alley because I had played football my entire life and that yardage was nothing for me to run.

The betters called out there man. Robert always put his money on me, he had watched me dust kids since I was in elementary school, so he knew that my odds to win him some easy bread was high.

Yancey Claxton, the Southside Gangstas and the Eastside Assassins all followed his lead-money on me. Chato Barnes put his money on Keith Spain from Dewey Street. Tariq Foster from the Northside brought his nephew Thrill Foster to get in the race. Dirty-D put his money on his niece Nicole Arnold my classmate. Before you knew it two-hundred dollars was on me to win.

I put my right foot on the crooked starting line, with the tip of my sneakers riding as close to the edge as possible. I bent my knees and readied my stance. I looked straight ahead of me, not to the side, not at my competition, but at the point man Byron Newberry who was standing 75 yards away from us with his hands in the air. Qwen Bell was the starter. She was Robert's little sister and she could be trusted to give a fair clean start. I memorized her cadence; the pace of her inflection was consistent and flowed easily out of her mouth.

"On ya mark"

"Set"

"Go"

***

My liking for Robert Bell and the fact that he always put his money on me made me feel good inside. Someone was depending on me to do my best, someone outside of my uncle and my football coaches. Even though I was sprinting to win him a purse of money, I wanted to do my best for him to come out on top of his friends.

I always gave my all in most of the things I did anyway, so this was no different for me. The word *GO* for me was a lightning strike. I don't have to tell you the rest of this part of the story, because you already know that I won that day and all the days after that. I had become Robert Bell's side-moneyman and one of his favorite little young dudes, which for me at that time was a good thing.

When I would win him that money, he would never give me any. Instead, he would take me the store and he would buy me and Donnie candy, Little Debbie Cakes, sodas and chips.

Thinking back on it now, I know why he did that. He didn't want me to have money in my hand to use as a weapon the way he did. He didn't want me to start to feel the vibe of gambling and having that powerful feeling of having a pocket full of money. He never let me have that type of experience with him. He would talk to me about my grades and would get mad if he heard that I got in any type of trouble.

As I got older and began my high school football career, he would sit in that same spot he always had when I was a boy, but this time instead of chilling with his women, he would be standing cheering me on. He had become an admirer of me, no longer wanting me to win a race for him, but now, he wanted me to win a race for myself. I would see him, Jayo, Billy and Fat Toney from time to time in the street but by then they had gained kingpin status in the drug game, so I kept my encounters with them brief for fear of becoming a victim once someone decided to kill one of them. Fat Toney barely spoke to me by that point-still holding on to things from a time long gone bye.

Donnie faded from my sight too. He made other friends and did other things that I had no interest in at the time. We rekindled our bond whenever were did link up, just like old times, which I appreciated. Donnie got killed a few years later after high school.

After that eighth grade summer, Robert Bell shut down the racetrack. My experience with him taught me how to compete in the street. There was no championship, no trophy to hoist up at the end of the game, no scholarship to earn, just running to win and having someone believing in you, even if it was a drug dealer.

I'm not one who makes believe
I know that leaves are green
they only change to brown when autumn comes around
I know just what I say
Today's not yesterday
and all things have an ending

-Stevie Wonder

2

2006 THE CIVIL WAR WAS YESTERDAY

BE EASY MY *friend.* The text message read. It came through about 4 a.m. from an unknown number. I turned off my notifications and silenced the ringer so I wouldn't ever be startled from my sleep again, something I never did before last year. But now, things were different, a lot different.

I no longer wanted to get messages in the middle of the night, not after what happened and I wouldna saw this one if I didn't have to get up to take a leak. My mind was damaged, possibly beyond any therapeutic repair, so I decided that if anyone needed me that early in the morning then maybe whoever it was should call the police before they called or text me. I was tired of helping. I was tired of being the one to always have to respond.

My phone rested on the stand next to the bed. My alarm clock was set for 5:30 a.m. and I chose the most disturbing alarm sound that Verizon had to offer on their list of tones.

***

(BRRRRRIIIINNNGGG!)

(An alarm clock clanged in the dark and silent room. A bed spring creaked. A woman's voice sang out impatiently: "Bigger, shut that thing off!")

That is who I feel like today, like Bigger Thomas, I thought to myself, re-playing the first lines I memorized in the 1940 novel Native Son.

These are the words that are trapped in my head, segments of a book…they echo like a bell at the top of the old church down the block. I had read this novel so many times, taught it more times than that, so much so that in a sense, I felt like I personally knew Bigger Thomas.

His life wasn't too much different from my own. He grew up poor and so did I. He had to kill mice and rats in his house and so did I. He loved his family and so did I. The separating factor was that I wasn't a criminal like him but I sure could have been. He let his situation force him down a road where the mud was so thick that he found himself stuck, sucked down so deep and unable to turn around.

I woke up with vague memories of the dream I had last night, but now it is all dawning, now it's all coming to light.

Lately, I have been haunted, by vultures and recurrences to a time I wish I could forget but I can't seem to duck those gunshots that shot past my head or dry the chocolate milk I spilled on my shirt when I was ten.

Looking out my window the gold-green and red-orange leaves reflect like the stained- glass windows of that church where we honored him before the darkness swallowed him whole. Of all the things I still remember, last autumn will never look the same.

I took the time to feel the temperature change around me, the summer's heat was disappearing and the once muggy wind was now kissed with the coolness of a winter slowly blowing its' way into town.

Like I said, I live with mental vultures and I had real reasons for feeling this way, because I got a slight condition, nothing life threatening from what the doctor said, but when it's happening it scares me into impending doom, so in my dreams it's actually easier to live, ducking bullets and trying to dry chocolate milk.

This house is old, drafty in more places than I can afford to insulate. The window next to my bed sticks because it's off track and can only open about four inches. A sticky four inches was just enough height to let a slight breeze press across my face. Four inches was just enough to breathe in the city's misery. Maybe, I thought, if I could get it back on track and if I tried to lift it any higher, five, six or seven inches, then that would blow more fucked up adjectives that I live around every day: hopelessness, poverty, and suffering and I didn't want that gusted into my window. Sounds crazy I know. It's even crazier that I won't go out and buy new windows like a regular thinking person with a good job would do, but to be honest, I like these old tattered sashed ones. They remind me of back in the day, old, but still strong after all these years gone by.

It has been months for me, getting out of this routine of checking-up on him. Him-I hesitate, to say his name. They say time heals but not really. For me, time has been nothing but a clock of ticking torment or what I can only imagine, of how being on death-row feels. You know, living in a cage like an animal, unable to hop the fence and run a sprint to a better place. There could only be so much imaging about what life is like on the freedom side without sorta going crazy.

When he was alive, I would wake up at 6:10 in the morning, grab my phone off this lopsided nightstand next to my bed, and call him, to make sure he was up and getting ready for school.

Somedays, when his grandparent's patience was lost, they would send him to me, to stay for a few days, sometimes a few weeks. He would sleep in the spare room, my old room, in the back of my house. I can still see him slowly deliberately walking up my driveway carrying his Southside Warriors bag on his shoulder that he used for a makeshift suitcase.

But this routine, which at one time I thought was good, was now broken down, like some of the houses on this street-off track like my window, you could say-it was dead-like he was dead, this routine that I had grown so used too.

For the first time, I woke up without him in the uppermost of my mind. It was strange, feeling this way, for now my life is back to just me, only worrying about myself. I have no more extra groceries to purchase. I have no football gloves or cleats to buy. Now, maybe, I can turn that room into an office or just keep it bolted shut forever locking away any memory of him.

Three hundred and sixty five days and some change has gone by since I saw him lying there dead-that early Saturday morning, face down, in that puddle of mud with water almost up to his ears. His football helmet sitting up erect as the rain beaded off the white shell washing down across the emblem. His headphones, the left one still stuck in his ear and the right, floating like a tiny boat navigating around his head.

Those three white cops hovering over his body, as he lay at their feet, while they talked and laughed, as they would do around a coffee pot in a police station breakroom, more worried about their feet getting wet than anything else. That is how casual they appeared to be, all the while, his white t-shirt soaking up the dirty water that was swirling around his bloody head.

Off in the distance Police Officers Romano and Jameson stood talking under the awning of the abandoned paint-chipped blue concession stand that sat obscured in darkness from a time long gone bye.

Homicide pulling and wrapping the yellow tape blocking off a fresh crime scene as the detectives scrambled around collecting what evidence that was available to them.

The Forensic Photographer capturing every angle of his body, his crossed legs, his right arm behind his back, his head-face down.

The slow moving paramedics, both black, bent low under the yellow tape, walking over to his body without an ounce of urgency. The one lifting up this dead boy's head from the puddle, his open eyes blinded by death and mud. The other opening up his medical bag to perform CPR, which would just serve as procedure and nothing more. Both obviously numb to seeing dead black kids.

Mr. Hall, the custodian, sobbing uncontrollably as he paced back and forth in the rain with no one to console him other than the detectives who questioned him as a suspect, not caring that he was given the task from God, to be the first to come upon the lifeless body under the bleachers.

The Browbow family huddled under an umbrella squeezing each other tighter than I assume any other time before.

This reoccurring dream that I keep to myself. *Fog hovering at eye level, about ten feet off the ground. I snatch my all black hoodie from off the back of my neck. I hop in my car and drive to the stadium, only a few minutes up the block and around the corner. It's always 2:35 a.m. when I get to the stadium. I get out and walk up to the locked gate. I unlock it and push it open across the uneven gravel driveway. The sound of those rocks have been with me since I played here. I close the gate behind me and lock myself inside. Sirens sound off in the night, but tonight it's quiet, eerily quiet. It's Tuesday night, in the hood and the silence was winning.*

I walk up the driveway until I reach the spot where they found Yosef's body lying, in a part grave-part grass area under the home side bleachers. My feet grasping the edge of the sunken spot of land where the weight of rain water has indented the ground. I stand there not moving, just starring down at his body that is there but not there, his face totally submerged under the puddle of water in this circular indented patch of grass.

I try to wake myself up but can't. I am convinced that I needed to be here, to visit this place at this hour, alone in the darkness of the shadows. I stand for a few more minutes. I begin to pray over the hallowed ground, then I turn and walk away. I unlock the gate, push it back across the gravel, closed it, lock it and drive away.

That is the movie I can't get out of my head, those are the images that cause the dreams that cause the pain so deep inside my guts, all over a dead black boy.

Football is a sanctuary for kids, especially the poor ones, the abandoned ones and the ones looking for a friend. They come seeking but not knowing exactly for what. The coaches provide this for them, a safe place away from their troubles.

Yosef had found peace but now this place of a safety had become his tomb, a small patch of indented of grass. Yet, this movie was real, there was no director screaming "cut" to end the scene, this script would act out to the end.

The rain was unsteady. Tilted with periods of deafening thunder and lightning that flashed the city back into daylight accompanied with heavy eye squinting rain. Then back to a soft nearly silent pitter-pat of raindrops diving into pools of gathered water on the grass and concrete.

It rained all four quarters of the game. I had been wet for hours but that rain seemed to be specific, aimed by the devil himself for us to witness, a moment of death, sadness and fear.

All of that, all of this time, these dreams and images, adding in with all the other demons that already dwell in my thirty-four year old mind, and it's a wonder that I ain't killed myself just to escape from myself.

Thirty-four ain't a long time to be alive, and it sure ain't long enough to be thinking about being dead. But here I am contemplating removing myself from the planet, I can't just blow my brains out, or take a handful of pills, or hang myself with a cord, because he needs me still-I guess, or maybe it's me that needs him. Killing myself…what would that do to the kids I work with. What would that do to Adrienne?

Things I cannot grab and kill-the ghosts that float around me, preoccupy me. They torment me and mock my every step.

***

It was autumn, the start of football and the one thing that was a constant in my life and was always precious to me since my youth and what I thought, would always hold a distinctive place in my heart, but now it seemed sour.

My mans' calling me sun because I shine like one,
and I rise before your eyes, and blind like one.

-Masta Ace

3

THE GHOST UNDER THE FLOOR

***(LIGHT FLOODED THE** room and revealed a black boy standing in a narrow space between two iron beds, rubbing his eyes with the backs of his hands. From a bed to his right the woman spoke again)... Native Son*

I paid crackhead George two-hundred and fifty dollars to refinish the wooden floors, something he learned when he worked for Floor Star Refinishing, before he was strung-out on the latest drug. We coated it with gym floor polyurethane so it shined like glass.

I rented a backhoe and George dug a trench around the base of the house and we sealed up every crack and broken brick to waterproof the basement and framed in glass block windows as deterrents to burglars.

I bought new appliances for the kitchen: a blender, a microwave, a stove and a refrigerator and modernized the bathroom with subway tile from wall to wall, a new water efficient American Standard Toilet and pedestal sink. The rest of the house I always made an excuse to do it another day, another year. The few things that I did complete made a nice gesture of my efforts that at least I was trying to make it my own.

My bedroom, which used to be my uncles, was located in the front of this one-story house, separated by a short hallway that stepped over into the living room. From there it branched off to the kitchen that spilled into a small back bedroom of my growing.

I had a queen-sized bed with a medium firm mattress and an antique Tiffany Lamp and two good, but used, sitting chairs in each corner. An 8x10 tightly woven Persian rug situated itself the middle of the floor, close enough to the bed for my feet to land on during cold mornings. I painted the worn, but effective, cast iron steam radiator old gold to help brighten the room.

Some of the things I left intact from when my uncle held post in here was due to my sentimental behavior that I had for objects that were dear to my heart and head.

My uncle's brass four-hooked coat stand that he found at a yard sale for twenty dollars. His two gold cufflinks that he won shooting dice behind a liquor store and his hardly creased wing tipped Stacy Adams shoes that still sat in the boxes. The black ones were my favorite.

His memories and life in the United States Army. The issued fatigues and combat boots, his rings and watches, the black amulets he wore for protection, the black beads that draped his neck, and the gloves he wore with the fingers cut out, and his "slave bracelets" made out of boot strings, the black power cane, which was just a stick with the nub carved into a clenched fist. Those things, he said were worn as direct insubordination toward the United States Army.

Insubordination was important to my uncle, as crazy as that sounds it really was important.

The most important object from my uncle that was in my possession was his red diary. That red diary to me was Christ's Holy Grail. I had it in my hands, in my safety. I had to protect it with my life, this small book, made of paper, written in ink and thumb-bent pages from when my uncle would read over the notes he wrote about his life all hidden safely within pages of a three-by-four leather cover.

***

In 1962, my uncle, his two friends, Jabo Wright and Tayloe Brooks caught a Greyhound Bus to New York City to see Malcolm X speak. He said there were thousands of people but they managed to bump their way to the front of the crowd and was in arm's length of shaking Malcolm's hand. Malcolm's speech that day was on economic empowerment and their wallets needed a boost.

My uncle was a watcher of movement, posture, body language and details of why a man does as such. He mastered that skill in the war but first learned it on the corners hanging out as a kid. In the hood posture is crucial, a lean too far to the left meant this. A lean too far to the right meant that. The way a man walked or when he walked and whether his hands were relaxed or clenched. Being able to recognize those small gestures could save your life and if not, it could cost it.

So that day he studied Malcolm as Malcolm sat on stage before his speech began; he said he frequently reached into his left lapel pocket to pull out a diary-a red diary.

He watched him write in it several times during that day and would always say to me when we would discuss the life of Malcom X that he wondered what he wrote on those pages. He said that day was special to him and what it told him was, that-a man should write things down, important and maybe not so important things and not rely solely on his memory.

Three years later in 1965 Malcolm X was assassinated. He was giving a speech at the Audubon Ballroom in Harlem when three gunman opened fire on him, killing him in front of his wife and children. Killed by his own kind, by one of ours, by brothers who were not really brothers, but a killers of X, the-man.

Malcolm's red diary, lay bullet riddled in the left breast pocket of the suit he was wearing and from that day on, my uncle carried his own red diary and now I am to care for it as my own.

***

In the basement, directly under the kitchen is a comfortable, just about finished man-cave. This room is where all my money and attention went. I was handy enough that I could do basic plumbing and carpentry, so what I could do with my hands and not have to pay a professional to do-I did it. Anything else that was out of my skill range I knew enough people who would do side jobs for merely no money, a carton of cigarettes, directions to the dude who sold weed, or the connect to the connect to get a few crack rocks. I couldn't help who I knew but I used it to my advantage whenever I could.

This room was special to me, not because it would soon serve as my ultimate chill spot but because it was where my uncle went back to the war-in his mind. Back then, under the surface of the ground, he was calmed sitting or sleeping in the dank coldness on a foldout cot and a tattered worn-out reclining chair. I hated being in this room back then but I was his only audience except when Jabo Wright would stop bye to share his moonshine that he kept tucked away under a towel as he would jog from his car to our backdoor.

The dampness of the walls and floor that now hid behind waterproofed cement and paint, the centipedes and spiders that would sit soundlessly with us as he talked about Dak To over and over again. It was like the needle at the end of the record.

At the back of our house there was a back door that either lead you up to the kitchen or down into the basement. At the bottom of the stairs under a broken ceiling light was a black door on the left and an open entrance on the right. The room on the right is where the washer and dryer was-both leaned to one side-both worked but made loud noise. It was also the room where clothes lay piled up wet with mold and stains that looked more like piss than anything else. The smell of rust was all around. The floor always seemed wet and you could hear a constant gurgle from the drain that sat in the middle of the floor.

The lighting was dim, evenly dark from wall to wall, crevasse to crevasse. One rear window selfishly giving a dirt-fogged view to the petite backyard but even during the day, though bright beams of sunlight could managed to shine their way inside; it never seemed to be enough.

The door to the left was the door to another world, another place and time. It was off limits to me unless my uncle allowed me to go in. He spent the majority of his time in here, in this underground safe place, talking to himself, talking to me, laughing with Jabo, but most time alone in the solace of summer, winter, spring and fall. His entire life behind a painted black door. This place was a gloomy blackened tomb; my young mind described it that way. My uncle's mind flashed back across the ocean to a place of his horror, a dreadfulness that began to replay when descended down eleven basement stairs.

Muted darkness was all around. The rugs had seen better days, years of wear and tear thinned them out exposing the floor underneath. Camouflage nets hung on the walls in places where painted pictures should be and wood grained liquor sat in bottles on the boxed window ledge adding an amber haze when the sun shined through.

Records in alphabetical order in old milk crates were stacked four feet high. His favorite group was called 21st Century, favorite songs were "Remember the Rain and Does Your mama Know." He would play those two songs every day and I ended up liking them probably as much as he did. Parliament-Funkadelic stayed in heavy rotation and by the time I was in high school I knew what funkentelchy meant.

My uncle, Kay-kee Smith, had a mental disorder from the war, way before psychologist called it PTSD. The black folks on the street just called him a "crazy niggah," but he was far from crazy, he was just ill-mentally. And that was his reason for wanting to be down in this dark room.

Most of the time he could keep it in check, but when he couldn't, times were bad around the house and that was why being in a bedroom close to the back door was the safest place for a little boy like me.

I was always on alert, Jabo Wright told me to be, Jabo said pray that his mind never created the illusion me as a Vietnamese "gook" instead of his black nephew and blow my head off or choke my little neck until it broke. I figured if anything jumped off then I could bust out the back door and run, run, run.

***

He was a "blood." The "bloods" as they called themselves were black men who were drafted into the Vietnam War between 1967 to 1970. Most of them were influenced by the teachings and politics of Stokely Carmichael, the black panthers and of course Malcolm X. My uncle was no different. He was a part of the "De Mau Mau Bloods," of the United States 1st battalion, 503 Infantry at Dak To, 1967. His blood name was 'Klick-Klack' for the two-letter K's in his name and the sound of his favorite weapon the Ithica 47 pump action shotgun.

He explained to me one day as we sat in the darkness, that, the De Mau Mau was formed for protection, not against the Vietnamese who were their so-called obvious enemies, but against the white soldiers within their own battalion but the Mau Mau Bloods at Dak To were hated by the Vietnamese people too, the same people they came to help.

Many of the white boys were from the Deep South and they openly and proudly boasted of their affiliation or legitimate membership in the Klu Klux Klan and the flying of the Confederate flag. To offset the oppressive ubiquity, the Mau Mau flew red black and green flags from their patrol boats and jeeps, and created a coded handshake called "dap," the same "dap" black people use today.' Those handshakes communicated messages, times and warnings to keep them safe and attentive within a place where they should have felt a sense of that anyway.

The ingenuity they had to have had to create a coded language in the most desperate of times the black soldier had been under since the Civil war.

My uncle's worst day was not fathomable in my insane-ist mind or up to that point from anything I had seen on TV or the big screen. "THE DEATH OF ORPHEUS FORDHAM" is how he always stared off this story. The way he described it to me the first time around was unbelievable as we sat in the musty air of that concealed basement.

He and Orpheus Fordham sat low under the brush of a tree. Orpheus had dozed off as his M-16 lay across his lap. My uncle said he let him sleep because he said O's wife had just informed by him letter that she no longer wanted to be married. My uncle figured that any man, who just got that kinda news, needed any break he could get. My uncle obliged him sleep to ease the fatigue of what was happening to him 8000 miles away.

As O slept, groups of farmers were walking from the interior of Dak To up to a large valley of hills for safe shelter from the many battles that took place in the Kon Tum Province. As they passed, one of the farmers jumped out of the caravan, ran up to Orpheus and with one swing of a machete chopped his head off. My uncle said time stood still and all around him fell into slow motion and that all he could hear was the wind traveling through the canals of his ears. He sat frozen until O's head rolled and bumped into his left leg. Vomit rushed up his throat but he held it back as it tried to erupt from his belly, he lifted his M-16 and killed the farmer with a bullet to the throat. He turned and kneeled over O's head and the farmer gurgled on his own blood in the background.

In this basement, in this moment my uncle stood up, holding an invisible gun like an air guitar and slowly sank down to the floor sitting on the back on his knees as if he was transported in a time-machine into the tall grasses of Vietnam again and like an actor in stage play, he cupped his hands as Orpheus's head rested in them. The details were vivid as he told me this true tale as I folded up deeper into the maroon recliner chair I remember sitting. His mind, he said-deteriorated on the spot and would never regained its normalness.

I often wondered what horrors my uncle's mind had locked away about his dear friend Corporal Orpheus Fordham.

***

400 West Glenaven is my street address, Southside, up the hill. The phrase 'up the hill' was an identifier for the residents on this side of town. If you lived on Sherwood, Princeton, Laclede, Dewey, St. Louis, Chicago, Earle, Glenaven, Evergreen, Regent, Warren, Cohassett, Delason, Balsam Ct, Willis, Chalmers, Marion, Cleveland, Kenmore or Myrtle then you were 'up the hill.'

When you ran into a dude you didn't quickly recognize but had an idea that he might be a Southside dude, you greeted him as such. "Where you from?" and if he said, "I'm from down the hill," then that meant that he was he had to live on Garfield, Breaden, Carroll, Falls, Parkwood, Lakewood, Woodland, Ridge, New Ct, New Ct Place, Hawthorne, Joseph, Werner, Hoffman, Edwards, Fairview, Plum, Mercer, School, John, Petrie, Wallace, Bernard, Granite, Rockview or High Street. Once you crossed High Street, you crossed over to the Northside of town which bled you into the Eastside which for us was off limits.

***

My next-door neighbor on the right of my house was a man named Douglas Dubois Brinson and on the left, a bando house on the verge of falling down.

Mr. Brinson's house was beautiful. Beautiful like the first day of a warm spring or like the inside of a car with new leather seats. His grass appeared to never grow and was green as green could get; the outer edges of his yard were lined up which in this neighborhood was a telltale sign of giving a fuck about your yard. The flowers that flanked each side of the gray front steps danced in rhythm to the slightest gust of wind. Baby blue and white paint dominated the color pallet of the wood siding and trim of the windows. The concrete driveway held no weeds as prisoners or cracks as hostages. His garage stood tall and looked as polished as the house. On one of the side walls was a twenty yard tool rack that held a long-wide rake, a spade and flat shovel, a weed eater and hedge trimmer. A red wheel barrel sat in the corner with ready to plant autumn mums that would soon join the family of other shrubs and flowers that decorated the front of his home.

On the inside of his house, crayon colored illustrations made by grandchildren blessed the entryway walls giving the guest a gallery feel upon coming through the front door. Portraits of his kids hung in a row along with their high school diplomas and college degrees. The pride of his family on display.

The living space had stylish furniture strategically placed at forty-five degree angles for adequate walking room from one chair to the next.

Black figurines of angels, and black and white photographs rested in aged patina frames that stood upright on an antique wooden coffee table centered on a slate gray plush rug.

The kitchen boasted of cleanliness that even the most interested mouse would not feel comfortable setting up camp. Each time I would go inside, I would leave more impressed than the last. His house was what I wished my house was, but it wasn't-not even close. I wished I had pictures of my family on the walls all smiling and hugging in laughter-but I didn't.

A bank foreclosure sat on the left of me, abandoned, going on three years as of last week. The owner whom I had only seen once or twice turned this property into section-8 housing. I wasn't too far gone into black middle class life that I didn't have sympathy for a family who needed government assistance, but I could not help but let it annoy me. It annoyed me because I'm on family number five within this three-year time span. Each of the five bringing a different set of family dynamics or let us just be real about it; dynamics is a code word for saying "problems."

Family number one had three kids all under the age of six which wasn't that bad for real, family number two had teenagers who didn't like going to school so their porch turned into a hangout of weed smoke, foul language and constant visitors, family three was just a single dude who tried his hand at turning the residence into a crack house, 4 and 5 was just a combination of one, two and three.

Therefore, seeing no one walking around over there on two legs was actually a relief for me. I had grown used to watching families of raccoons live in luxury, along with every stray dog and cat who needed a cozy spot to take a nap, a shit or both.

I would walk inside at least twice a month, not sure why, I figured maybe to see something different from one week to the next, which to be honest, was exactly what I would see. The steps got creakier, the porch boards more worn down to the bare exposed wood, the gutters bending down to see who would be the first to touch the top of the untrimmed bushes. The door leaning off the hinges holding on with one less bolt that gravity pulled out of the door jam. The gang graffiti spray paint, some with skilled artistry but most with a kindergartener's effort. Aerosol nicknames outlined in black pigment, Man-Man, Paco, Killa-K overlapping letters and streaks of random strokes of planned out colors.

The smell of human piss, animal hair and dead mice enflamed the air. Crack pipes, syringes and needles scattered across the lopsided floor over the waterlogged carpet. Disregarded furniture and mattresses that didn't find their way onto the back of a U-Haul truck took up space in the middle of the first room.

The kitchen looked like an episode of the TV show Hoarders, cups, plates, old cereal boxes, macaroni packs, broken sticks of spaghetti, bugs of all kinds, some still crawling but most dead in a rigor- mortis state. Drip-dried rust stains on the side of the electric stove that no longer had a plug to bring it back to life, the white refrigerator lying on its' back, doors open to the world waiting to be resuscitated by the junkyard paramedics.

The bando on the left and Brinson's palace on the right and my house a mixture of both in the middle.

At the corner, on my side, was a set of small brick apartments called The Denison Villa. The Den as we called it housed all types of black people, mainly the types that meant no good. When I was young, it accommodated young white and black couples who shared working downtown in common. Now it was a haven for black trouble or trouble for a black, however you wanted to look at.

Glenaven, a street that once had a family in every house was now a wasteland of bandos, a few lived in houses, separated by empty lot after lot, like gaps in a picket fence.

Across the street from the Denison, was a neighborhood establishment called the 5th Avenue Bar & Grill. The name of the bar never made sense to me because there were no streets identified by number on the Southside.

That was my uncle's hangout spot. During the summers, I would walk up there with my friends and stand in the doorway, waiting for the bartender, Ms. Evelyn to come to the door and give us chilidogs and Pepsi Colas to drink. My uncle didn't mind us doing that as long as we didn't step foot inside. Ms. Evelyn was digging on him anyway.

***

Mr. Brinson was my uncle's friend and my self-appointed caretaker after my uncle passed, even though he didn't have to be, seeing that I was fully grown now, but I welcomed it out of respect. He had a key to my front door and used it a few times when he thought I may have committed suicide or fell victim to neighborhood criminals'. One day, he keyed his way right into the middle of me and a woman having sex on my couch. After that, he was a little more conscience of just coming over uninvited-you shoulda saw the look on his face.

My uncle gave him that key when I was a kid, probably for the same reasons, suicide or murder. I know that Brinson knew about my uncle's mental state-of-mind, so that made sense back then, but he must have thought that through osmosis that-that syndrome crept into my brain as well.

He was a short round man with glasses and rusty hands from years of hard work. His hair was grey, slicked back to middle of his head, almost fully covering the bald spot that worked hard to be exposed. His skin was bronze and still had enough youthfulness in his face to see that at one time he was truly a handsome younger man.

He was always up early working on his yard. He was old school like that, you know, the importance of a manicured front yard to some black people. He made me feel guilty about not cutting my grass on time, or chasing away the section-8 animals that lived left of me.

His tool of choice this morning was a gas leaf blower. I watched him out of my window hurling leaves from the oak tree through the white balusters onto the front yard.

I anticipated his morning greeting. He memorized my morning schedule as another way to keep track of me.

"Who are we playing this week AJ?" he asked me projecting his voice toward my four-inch open window that was parallel to his front porch.

"Rayen," I answered with my face nearly pushed on the window screen so he could hear me.

"Rayen Tiiigggggers?" he said in an animated voice.

"Yep Rayen, it's a big game too probably for the league championship," I said, as I tried to keep my voice aimed toward the screen, while at the same time trying to get dressed.

"Boy, I can recall whooping up on them many-many-years ago, and then watching your uncle shoot the lights out the gym, killed them every time, boy, he sure could shoot the lights out of a gym," he said.

We used to beat them in football and basketball. The only player that gave your father some competition was Floyd Showers, now he was good."

But that was when the school was damn near all-white, this neighborhood too, matter of fact, my family, Ida Brown and a black couple…the Managualt's, was the name, were the only black families on this block, but they only stayed here a few months. We never really got to know them because they let them white folks run them off this street."

I heard parts of this story before over the years during our morning salutations each time helping me piece together the history of this street and neighborhood I live in

"I was just a boy, me and my brothers and sisters were the only black kids on this whole street. The Managualt's stayed right there, at the end down there, they didn't have kids. Right there next to Mrs. Ida's old house."

I knew exactly where he was pointing too; it *was* right next to Mrs. Ida's old house. Ida Brown gave me my first job. The thought of her always made me smile. Her and her husband were from North Carolina and moved to Ohio with the northern migration of black folks. When they bought a house on this street "white flight" began. They didn't have any kids and her husband had died from a busted appendix. My uncle who was chivalrous saw this as an opportunity for me take a step into my manhood, so he walked me to her house one morning and had her hire me as her landscaper, garbage man and cleanup crew.

My uncle requested that my employment be done for free but Mrs. Ida insisted that I should be paid for my service, which I gladly agreed with. We negotiated five dollars to cut the grass every two weeks, one dollar to take the trash can to the curb and the cleanup was no charge.

When I mowed her lawn as she would walk behind me, making sure I didn't miss a blade of grass or roll over any of her flowers and if I did, she would walk me back down to my house, tell my uncle and that five dollars quickly turned into two dollars and fifty cents. That was my job all the way up to the twelfth grade.

Time seemed to fly bye. I grew up and Mrs. Ida's hair was now graying over her temples. All those years of being near her and not ever realizing that she had become a missing piece in my life. She had become the mother figure that I needed. The summers of being in the hot sun with her sitting on her porch as she watched me bag grass talking to me about my life, school and the world around me. The youngness of my mind to simple to see that she was working for me like I was working for her, but she was doing God's work-loving me.

Years later, when I was in college, she died in her front yard tending to her garden. I came home for her funeral. I sat next to Mr. Brinson, he said it was a fitting place for the old girl to give up the ghost. Not sure how, but I guess that's how he saw it. After she was put in the ground I went home and sat with Mr. Brinson on his porch. He went inside and returned with a long box. “

Antietam Mrs. Ida told me to make sure you got this, she told me to hold on to it until you were old enough to respect it and appreciate it,” he said.

I lifted off the top and the box was full of comics from front to back. I fingered through them as my eyes held back tears.

“This was her husband’s collection,” Brinson said.

“And she said to give it to me?” I asked.

“Yes, she did.”

I pulled out each book one by one and carefully softly slid each one back down into its place.

“This is where your uncle got that Luke Cage from, he bought it off of Mr. Brown for you when you a little boy.”

***

My father wasn’t scared of the white man.” Brinson said snapping me out of my daydream about Mrs. Ida and the long box of comic books.

“They tried to run us outta here but he wouldn’t go. He had a job in that steel mill like most of the black men did during those times. He bought this house with his own money, paid it off and left it to his children.

I remember we would get dressed for church and pile up in the car, and he would tell us not wave at nooo-byedee unless they waved at us first. Yep-my daddy didn’t take no mess, proud man, yes sir.

See, I always liked this street, even with all the white folks on it. It was better than where we were before, over there off the Sharon Line in the Victory Projects with all them black folks. Because if you know like I know Antietam, that every brother, not a brother. So when dad and mother passed on, and we were all grown and moved away, I decided to bring my family back into this same house and make it our home, been here ever since.”

Talking to Brinson always takes me to the beginning and my years with my uncle. The early mornings, when I used to wake up tired from football practice, looking at the Jet Magazine Beauties of the

Week taped on the backside of my closet door. That was my first experience with girls, some scotch tape and the last page of a five by seven magazine.

I can still hear his voice coming under my door… *"Ey boy, let's get moving, can't be late going to school."* The brash sounding dialect is just as clear today in my ears as it was all those years ago.

I used to rush to the bathroom to avoid hearing more of his yelling and to be first to the over worked bar of soap that he and I shared.

Running across these once threadbare wooden floors, hearing the clink-clank of his United States Army issued utensils that he brought back from Nam, two metal dented plates, bent forks and spoons and two drinking cups-one with a bullet dent pressed in it. We were straight prison style, no fancy saucers or tableware, just raw steel and an undressed two-person formica table.

The fragrance of hot eggs and beef bacon balanced in the air. There was no pork ever in his house. My uncle subscribed to the black man and pork don't mix dietary law. My friends used to laugh about that and always made sure to let me see the big pork ribs they were allowed to eat on the regular.

Yeah, that '*tink*' sound from the spoon hitting the metal, sounding the alarm that it was time to eat.

The meek looking furniture that surrounded the 12x10 living room made it a home for us. The oak mantelpiece where his varsity letter rested that he earned with his big hands, bouncing and shooting a basketball, overlapped by two black and white photographs of him in Vietnam, the war that took him away at nineteen years of age. The diary he kept with all his notes, numbers, thoughts and feelings.

In my eyes my uncle was King Kong- a giant of a man in height and personality. He was 6'4 or so. He weighed about 190 pounds and had dark almond brown skin that housed scars from his time in the streets and from hand-to-hand combat in the war. He was handsome and cool. He wore his short afro pushed back with a crisp razor-sharp lineup. He dressed like what I would call 'regular', nothing flashy or fancy, manly is the best word for it. He wore Army fatigues whenever he had the chance.

He dated a few women at the same time, but he never let them get to know him well enough to ever move in, or get overly comfortable and maybe think to try to start mothering me, or trying to be a wife to him. He would let a few quick conversations from them penetrate my ear depending where she was ranked on his list other than that I was off limits to them.

He was cognizant, that it was the war that fucked up his head and every thought that tried to stay in proper balance. It made him what white people or the conservative black would call "militant," but to me, he was just frustrated, desperate to be what this city considered a *normal* person. I watched him fight his mind and lose and those loses put him on his back more times than not. To see a man get knocked down metaphorically was harder than seeing him literally on his knees in pain, a pain that I had no idea a man could suffer, but one that I would soon fall victim too.

Nevertheless, what really destroyed him, was seeing what heroin had done to his friends and his only sister, my mother. He looked at all that as the same thing, something that the government did to his people. He would bang his open hands on the table, loosening up the four wooden legs that tried their best to stand strong under the pressure of his heavy palms.

"How will I stand, if you turn out the light that shines over me?" he would mumble in his darkness creating a haunting echoing sound that traveled up through the cracks and gaps of the wooden boards in my room. I remember laying down with my ear pressed to the floor taking in the hypnotizing chant. It scared me.

My uncle was the ghost that lived under the floor…

All I do, I do it for you. It's for all you did, when I was a kid
Cause there's mad friends ain't wanna be born
But I'm glad to be the son of Yvonne.

-Masta Ace

4

1981 Magdalene

MEMORIES LIVE IN my mind of the affection and appreciation I had for my uncle Kay-kee Smith. He blessed me with the small things that the average person might take for granted-like giving love from a man to a boy, an uncle to a nephew or making sure I always had grape jelly for my toast because he knew it was my favorite. My appreciation for him was as deep as Atlantis because he was all I had to love.

Memories live in my mind of the conversations we shared-this one in particular.

"We was down nephew-down in the bush," he said to me one day.

"What-chu mean Unc?" I asked him.

"We was down on our bellies...we had to get down and crawl on our forearms so we wouldn't get shot dead. The Viet Cong soldiers was some slick sneaky mutha-fuckas nephew. You stand ya ass up at the wrong time and get sniped-they could put a bullet right between your eyes, be coming back to the states in a body bag-right back to the hood to get buried.

Shit, I don't know what was worse: the Viet Cong or the swarming mosquitoes flying past my ears all day and night or them yellow sac spiders-one bite and your dead. I saw a white boy from Kentucky get his ass bit by a bamboo pit viper, snake jumped out of a tree like a green flash of lightning and clipped him right behind his ear. He screamed so loud it echoed through the trees, instantly we got fired on because his scream gave away our location. So many bullets rained on us, it ripped the leaves up like confetti at a parade. I was down on my stomach, he was lying in front of me I had to put my hand over his mouth… I knew that snake venom was running through his veins, you could see the fear of death in his eyes, you think this white boy cared about any of that shit that was going on…man this punk looks at me and grabs my hand off his mouth and says to me "get your nigger hand off me."

"For real?" I asked him.

"For real nephew, hear I am the only man that can maybe save his life and he worried about my hand because it's black.

So guess what I did…I crawled away from him and let his white ass die. I hoped the maggots, millipedes, centipedes and all the other creepy ass bugs had a feast on him."

"The war, the conditions of war, brought every strength and weakness in a man and the first weakness of man in that situation to show was a man's feet. A man with wet socks in the bush turns into a coward. Socks were like gold bars in the Federal Reserve Bank, every man wanted dry socks and the one who had them was the man who had the keys to the bank. That man could trade one pair of dry socks for almost anything he wanted or needed."

My uncle never took that little thing for granted and he carried those experiences with him his whole life and taught me the same-the importance of having dry socks. So when we were *down*, we never complained, when we didn't have a lot to eat or if the electricity got turned off from time to time, he and I had *socks* that we shared with each other. LOVE

***

Early mornings when football season came about, he would wake me up to get ready for my games. My game pants rested in the chair next to my bed, my cleats sat below with my socks rolled into a ball that he would place into one shoe. My jersey, he would put over my shoulder pads with my helmet inside the head hole. After I ate, he would walk me to my football games down to Rodgers Park.

Rodgers Park had two football fields, three tennis courts, a caged-in basketball court and two baseball fields that sat at the bottom of a hill next to the Rodgers Community Center. My team always met underneath the picnic pavilion at the far end of the park. There, we would make sure we all were dressed properly and that time was also used to see which kids had to go and get weighed in-112 was the cut off weight-113 meant you couldn't play that game.

The football fields were enclosed with a thick yellow wire that separated the crowd from the sidelines. There were no bleachers to sit in so that wire kept the antagonistic parents, uncles, aunties and the random adult men who coached from a distance from standing on the backs of the teams and coaches.

Two fields meant that two games went on at one time, so you can picture what it looked like every Saturday from 9 a.m. in the morning to 3 p.m. in the afternoon. The league had seven teams. The Southside Penguins, the Zulu Warriors, the Eastside Bulldogs, the Suns of Thunder, the Boys Club, the Buckeye Elks and the Hagstrom House Braves which was the team that I played on.

I can still see us walking, me holding his big hand. As we walked, I used to swing my helmet like a pendulum, something he hated. He used say that I looked like I was too happy to be about to go play a football game swinging my helmet like a friendly dog wagging his tail. When all it really was-was that, I was just happy to be with him.

He would spend our journey giving me a pre-game pep talk about not being scared to hit anybody as hard as I could. I would shake my head in agreeance, with a small scowl on my face trying to make him believe that I was tougher than I really was.

My position was Quarterback. I wore number 12. I loved playing football. I wasn't the biggest kid or the smallest on our team. I was in the middle. I could run fast and I had good jukes, and I wasn't afraid to run your over if I had too.

My coaches gave me the nickname was Bumblebee, but on my street, they called me Ant-short for Antietam or for my middle name Anthony but I liked Bumble Bee the best.

I loved everything about football, the contact, the dirt and the hot sun, but I especially loved our uniforms. Our colors were orange and white. We had orange jerseys, white helmets with an orange Michigan Wolverine logo spray painted on it. I wore white Sacony cleats and white tube socks with two orange stripes. Mrs. Brinson and Mrs. Ida used to say I looked cute in my uniform, my uncle hated when they said that because I would always smile. Probably, because I didn't know what else to do.

We had a band that played for us each game, the Hagstrom House Marching Band. The band had kids from the projects in it and the leader was a teenager named Sticks-With-A-Limp. He played the snare drum and was hype-man of the band. Every Saturday they led us from under the pavilion onto the field like a circus troop entering the Big Top. It was the image of a parade for us on game days. Those were the best times of my life when I was little boy.

***

On this Saturday was the first time I saw her. I was standing with my uncle and his friend Jabo Wright outside the yellow wire.

"You heard from your 'Sis' man?" Jabo asked him with his eyebrows raised.

My uncle looked around before he answered.

"Hell-nah man, and I hope I don't…I have seen her down here a few times with some niggah she runs with. I been ducking and dodging her because I don't want him to see her."

I was crowding my uncle with my shoulder pads poking him in his thigh, when this woman started yelling out his name as loud as an ambulance siren. I thought it was one of his girlfriends who was happy to see him again, or maybe hadn't seen him in a long time.

I remember how pretty this woman was. She glowed like crispy edges of golden hash browns. Her eyes were a dark opaque gray and her hair was the color of sepia brown like the mantle at our house, much how maybe a black angel would look-of course I didn't use those elaborate adjectives back then but if had that vocabulary at that age, that is how I woulda described her.

She wore glasses but was beautiful behind them, not ugly or plain looking like the girls in my class. Even as boy, my young eyes knew a beautiful face when I saw it and I could see that she was one that had an effect on my uncle. I thought she would make a good girlfriend, not that I really knew much about that, I just compared her to all the women he ran in and out of our house and she was the best to me. She fit what he liked I thought to myself at that time. But my uncle just stood there and never responded to her yells of "Kay-kee."

I looked up at him to see why he wouldn't answer her. She started walking towards us with her hips swaying side to side, he pulled me behind him, shielding me from her fast approaching steps as if she was about to steal me away or something.

She got within feet of us, when a man cut off her path. The man who intercepted her, she obviously had an acquaintance with; he touched her in places that only adults touched each other behind a closed door. He yanked her around like a rag doll without an attached head leading her away from where we stood. He reached into his pocket and gave her something that she immediately put in her mouth, at that time, of course, I didn't know what it was, candy I thought…I remember her smiling, like she liked being treated that way. But how could she, why would she?

I was peaking around my uncle's hip, his hand still locking me behind him, my chest pressed up against his thigh. My uncle took a few steps toward her dragging me along, but stopped. Jabo Wright had quietly pulled out a palm-sized pistol that he had hidden away in the small of his back. She kept looking over her shoulder as the man tugged on her harder and harder. He led her away off into the crowd.

She yelled out again, but this time she said, "I know you little boy-Kay-tell him who I am-tell him who I am."

My uncle spun me around in a fast about face and hurried me to the where the rest of my team was gathered. I tried to look back at her like Lot's wife must have in the Bible, but my head was palmed by my uncle's octopus sized hands, that turned me in the direction he wanted me to go.

I asked him who she was and before he could answer, Jabo jumps in to give his explanation. My uncle silenced him with his eyes. Jabo stepped back, with both hands in the air like a cop with a gun pressed to his spine, signaling retreat of overstepping his bounds.

"Nobody, just some woman I used to know," my uncle said in a quick.

I was engulfed in my youth and curious enough to keep fishing for information, and I knew that she, whoever she was-was just not some woman he used to know, but a person that I would soon find filled an empty place in my heart.

Later that evening, after I ate two hot dogs, a bag of chips and a Hug Grape Drink. We went outside and sat on the porch, the sun was setting, and it was the first time I really ever looked at the sun going down, my uncle took a long deep breath as his shoulders sank at ease. He looked into my young face and told me who she was to me. That day I never forgot, the day I found out about my mother.

***

As years passed, he divulged more information about her and their life together growing up, even things about who and where my father was.

Her full name was Lilly-Ann Smith, his only sister and yes-my mother. My grandparents were from Carrollton Georgia. My grandfather's brother, Ticket, disappeared one night on a dark road coming from a corner store, a store that was across some train tracks, which was the border to the white side of town.

My great grandfather swore that the KKK got a hold of Ticket and ended his young life, after that, my uncle said that his father-my grandfather, Thomas, who was thirteen at the time was sent to Detroit Michigan on a train, accompanied by a Pullman Porter who was her second cousin. He lived in Detroit for a year and got sent to Youngstown Ohio with his other brother Velt. Velt worked at United Steel in the Blast Furnace. The blast furnace produce coke fuel; Coke is a grey, hard, and porous fuel. The coal was baked in an airless oven, a "coke furnace" at temperatures as high as 2,000 °C. The blast furnace had black men of all ages working in there and that was because it had the hottest and harshest conditions in that part of the plant. My uncle said it was the closest thing to slavery conditions of the south. He said it was a subliminal punishment for black men, sticking them down there. My grandfather at fourteen years of age began his employment in that hell on earth of the blast furnace.

Years later, my grandfather sent for Grandmother Dee-his high school sweetheart and they became one in the union of marriage. My grandmother was in charge of the woman's Saturday School class at Building #7 of the Noble Drew Ali Moorish Science Temple. That was her pride and joy, teaching other woman how to live and study.

They had two kids, a boy named Kay-kee and a girl-Lilly-Ann. They lived down-the-hill behind the Oakhill Cemetery.

He said my mother got pregnant by what he called-a street niggah. She gave birth to me on a cold December night in 1971, never even held me in her arms, but demanded that the nurse give me to him to hold onto like a small brown paper bag of money.

I spent seven days in the hospital along with my grandparents, and my uncle in one room, and my mother in another, all of us waiting on my father to show. That wait was in vain. She checked out with no fuss and quietly went about her way.

They next time she was seen was with that same man who years earlier yanked her around. She promised my uncle that she would come back and get me when she was settled in (whatever that meant in her definition), all together finding herself all the way strung out and eventually boy-friendless. I guess, no man, wants, or needs, an out-of-her-mind junkie, even if he was the one who created the zombie. My uncle said, my mother at one time, was the prettiest woman he had ever seen, and when I think back to that one day that I saw her face, she was just that, the prettiest woman I had ever seen too.

My father's name is Ghee Watkins-Jones. He was originally from Chicago. My uncle ran into him sitting at a bar, called Foys Lounge over on Willis Avenue. He approached him about a girl named Lilly and her son. Ghee snickered and said to my Uncle, "what about that bitch?" Now, I didn't really have to hear the next part of this story, because I knew my uncle, blood got spilled, and not his, but Ghee's. Ghee Watkins-Jones got his ass kicked that night. My uncle made sure he understood that, he better not be seen again on the Southside and he wasn't.

According to my uncle, Ghee never loved my mother, it was that birds and bee's conversation that my uncle and me had when I got older, but the street version, that my mother was just another piece of ass to Ghee. Even though I really didn't know anything about that up to that point.

Ghee, I guess, figured himself to be a black gangster, a Youngstown El-Rukn and didn't have to time to father some random ass little boy like me when money had to made on the corners of

Youngstown. He had friends who still lived around here, and they knew I was his seed, and when they caught me alone in my growing up years, they would give me reports on his whereabouts, most of the time, it was jail or on the run. As I grew, I used to hope and pray, that he was some muscular man's "piece" in a jail cell or maybe lying dead in an alley, either one was okay with me.

Anyway, that left me, and my uncle to care for each other, him, a young war veteran, and his 'handed-over' nephew.

"Believe only half of what you see and nothing that you hear."

-Edgar Allen Poe

5
JABO WRIGHT

"HARD TO LIVE out here brotha, drugs destroyed our communities and turned our beautiful women ugly and our strong men into weaklings," Jabo said as he sat in the old recliner in the corner of our house. I was hiding behind the couch overhearing them talking.

Jabo Wright was my uncle's best friend. They had been friends since they were little and he was the other half of my uncle's 'crazy niggah' street reputation. He loved my uncle like a brother and had put his life on the line for him on more than an occasion.

Jabo was from the great lineage of Whites, not white people but from the last name of White. He carried the blood of the first black man to live in Youngstown, John White. John White was so well respected that each time Frederick Douglass would visit Mahoning County, Douglass would sit with him. They would discuss politics and the state of black Americans in the valley.

Over the years, the torment of being up from slavery, Jim Crow and the Black Codes that almost wiped out the black population in the Mahoning Valley, so his family somewhere along that timeline changed their last name from White to Wright, a blacker sounding name and a safer sounding name.

"A black man with dark skin with the last name White was a direct insult to some white folks back then." Jabo would say when he preached the history lesson of how his family ended up in Youngstown.

He was not as tall as my uncle was, but tall enough to as not to appear short standing next to him. He was long, wiry, in the arms, with short nappy hair and a rough stubble beard. His skin was dark, not blue black, but just black like coffee bean black.

His eyes were low like mine, with a slanted tilt. He wore fancy leather jackets and nice crown toe shoes in the winter and plush loafers in the summer. He always looked comfortable.

He walked with a slight limp because he got his leg crushed one night on the side of a road fixing a flat tire; the car slipped off the jack and smashed his right kneecap. And for that accident; he got a check every month for being unable to work, until Tayloe hooked him up with a custodian job at a metal fabrication factory so he always had money in his pocket. Jabo used his charm on the secretary at the factory to pay him in cash, so no paper trail could follow him as he cheated the United States Government out of that workers compensation money.

That bad leg kept him from Vietnam or ever walking upright again. I think he felt guilty for letting my uncle go to war without him, thus his possible over dedication to him. He had no wife or children but had a brother who was the city council member in Ward 9, and to have that in his back pocket not only kept him out of jail but always a step ahead of any changes that might affect his lifestyle. He had all the hook-ups and all the connections which he shared with my uncle.

"My nephew man…the shit pisses me off and I feel bad for him because he ain't got no mamma, all boys need a mamma blood."

"Maybe if you settle down, he might get a mamma," Jabo said.

"Man, that ain't gonna happen no time soon, even though I do like Monica a lot. She makes some good fried fish and that might be enough to marry her."

"Good fish don't make a good wife," Jabo said laughing.

"It don't hurt any."

Silence took over the room in what I guessed was my uncle thinking about being married and if Monica would make a good mother for me.

"That heroin turned my sister into a whore," my uncle said randomly.

I wondered, as I sat low in the dark of that couch, what the word "*whore*" meant, and then, years later, I learned the definition from my cousin Binky who was in high school at the time. It hurt me more than anything had up to that point, but I never heard any more bad things about my mother or ever wanted to for fear of that same hurt vomiting back up.

Thirty years ago, seems like forever, hiding behind that couch. I owe my uncle everything for making me who I am, a college graduate, a schoolteacher, a football coach, a man in the truth, a man who would take care of a kid like Yosef.

My uncle is long gone and now, Yosef too, but memories live.

There’s a war going on outside no man is safe from…

-Mobb Deep

6

SHS

ALL THIS REMENISCING got me running late for work. Now I'm rushing. Bullshit ass quick breakfast, grab my lunch bag and I'm out. Lucky for me the school is only down the street.

"Have a good day Mr. B," I yelled over the blare of the leaf blower.

Not letting me walk away, "close to that day ain't it?" He asked.

"Yes sir, it is, very close."

"Shame what they did to that boy… I know you miss him; he was a good young man- he was like a little brother to you."

"Yes sir, he was."

I rambled up to my truck door; put my bag on the passenger side. *Close to that day…shame what they did to that…*why did he have to say that shit to me? Ima walk to work today. I need the air. Those words that Brinson just said to me, got me vibrating with nervousness, making me think about shit I am trying to forget-you know-run away from.

***

My uncle loved being outside. He taught me to love it too and consider all the nature around me, not including the boarded up windows or the kicked in mailbox at the corner but also the people who walked over the fallen leaves crushing them into gold dust. The faces young with life and old with wisdom, some smiling, some with frowns. The black boys on the corner, no longer going to school, the black girls who ignore them on their way to first period.

During this walk Ima about to take, Ima consider the life my mother lived and the game this Friday and Yosef. Ima consider why things look so bad out here. Ima consider why I know-too many niggahs and not enough Black people. Ima consider, the women who walk their kids to school because I never got that chance to walk or hold my mothers' hand.

The sidewalk, uneven, broken, smooth, level, like a ghetto yellow brick road. Stray dogs that look at you and appear to laugh as they trot away, pit-bulls tied up in backyards on a thick unbreakable choke chains.

Consider all nature, anything outside is worthy to be looked at by human eyes. The birds that still make nest in the trees along the block. The deer who are out of place but are brave enough to nibble on the flowers that decorate front yards.

***

Youngstown Southside High School is where I teach and coach, is. It's an up-the-hill school and sits on one of the busiest streets in the city, Market Street.

Market Street is the gateway from the suburbs to downtown; it's a straight shot past the inner workings of the 'hood'.

Beware black boy who ain't down with the Southside ways, East-sider, North-sider you would be smart to stay on Market, because hazarding off it, whether on purpose or by accident, could be bad for his health, like death by bullet or beating by fists. If it's the formers, and it usually is, then no for a fact that he may come up missing and get found half dead in an alley or dumped on the Sharon-Line off in some sticker bushes. That cool cat from the other side of town, who calls himself digging on girl from Southside High and shows up at lunch or after-school to hold her hand in front of her friends, is not only brave, but also crazy. I was witness to that episode several times.

Then you got what I call the educated drug addicts. Those are the cars sun-glassed-out white boys who cruise our blocks during their lunch hours in their fancy cars on their way home from the university or from their suit wearing jobs, only do so to make a purchase of their favorite drug, and then ride away back to their luxurious homes, with trimmed lawns, smooth concrete streets and flattened walkways.

Then, you got us; black people like me, the ones who made good briefly ascending off this dead tree branch. Spending two to four years depending on how much money you had or how much your brain could take, enclosing yourself up in an institution of higher learning all for a paper degree, only to fall victim to the guilt of being formally educated and fly back to the dead tree. Then, mastering the art of holding down a job but still dabbling with weed or on occasion popping a quick pill on a Saturday night. All of that, still down on the darkest blocks, at the darkest times of night, with them vultures I see when I am asleep.

***

Black people have in innate characteristic to turn most places, dwellings, basements, backseats and porches into hangout spots. We mean no harm, it's just something we do to sooth our desperate need for fellowship in the midst of the chaos that surrounds us every day. That search for fellowship mixed with the devil and his overarching influence can turn the most honest starting endeavors into a place of mustiness.

Across from Southside High is a store, Rafedies Quik-Stop. Rafedies is sandwiched between two low-income apartments. There was a tight seven-space parking lot directly in front of the store. The occupants of the apartments had to park on the side street. The Quik-Stop owner was an Arab man named Rafedie Gamal. He was one of the first Arabs to settle and become an instant owner in my neighborhood. We didn't care twenty years ago, until it became apparent that the black residents of this same city would never be given the same opportunity to own a store, car lot, consulting firm or anything that needed to look white or foreign, to be patronized by people with money. As long as it did not have a tint or shade of black and brown then you could shake and move.

I happened to like Rafedie. He wasn't the problem. The location of the building was the source and cause of worry for anyone within a mile of its doors. That innateness I spoke about that we have brought bad company to the store. It became a place of loitering, a nightclub during the daytime. Students were in and out of the entrance at all hours that the sun shined, some for lunch, some to skip class and some just to stand.

***

We have our own language here. People from Chicago and Detroit call us country but we are far from the slang of the sticks. Our verbal milk is our own, nether old school, or new, it is a blend of all the words and sounds from hard work, poverty and love. We greet with head's that nod up and not down, a sign that you are from the YO. If you do it any other way then we know that you are either in implant or just a straight sucka.

When I approach the front door of the school, Officer Walter Jameson Sr. greets me each morning. He is the schools resource officer. We played ball together back in the day.

He sits at this dented metal desk at the top of the stairs of the entry door. It was his job to make sure traffic flowed up and down the stairs. The admin thought it was a good idea for the students to see the police first thing each day as they entered the school.

Jameson had been on the force since dropping out of college to raise his son after two years with an associate's degree in Criminology. I hated to say it but his badge made him. It was easy to see that his confidence came through the uniform he wore. He was always a weak-minded ego driven typa brotha.

Most of the students like him but then you had the ones who didn't show respect to his badge. Some didn't realize that he was a real police officer because he was posted up in the front stairwell every day, so that didn't compute with them, so they treated him with that security guard status. I thought it was funny. I knew that the disrespect that a few teenagers showed him bothered him.

Jameson spent Monday's, Wednesday's and Friday's in school from 9:30 to 2:30 and his Tuesday's and Thursdays eight hours on the street patrolling with his partner, an Italian man, named Joey Romano. I didn't like him. I really didn't like Jameson either to be honest, but I made sure Romano knew that I didn't like him. I let Jameson slide with how I felt about him because we were teammates on the '89' team and now, his son, Walt Jr. was our starting tailback.

Since we had a history, he used that to gain access to conversations with me about how to coach football and to publically second guess what we should have or should not have done in the games. Like I said before, I don't like him, I tolerate him to say it in a nicer way.

Every stadium has permanent fixtures, old ass men who come to every game, they sit in the same spot and say the same shit every game whether that shit is good or bad-it's always the same. I never had a problem with them old asses, it was the next generation that created all my game day headaches. Every Friday night Jameson stood next to Ole-man Bobby Cykes, who consistently heckled and criticized us. Bobby played here in the late seventies and went on to play pro ball in Canada. Somehow, along the way over the years Bobby Cykes became a voice against the program. Maybe it was because he didn't want any team to be better than his, seeing that they were the first to win three playoffs games in the school's history. I wasn't sure what his angle was but I do know that he applied to be the head coach before Coach Browbow got here but was turned down. I figured that Jameson was learning from one of the all-time best hecklers Southside had to offer. Fuck both of them.

***

On the street, Jameson's reputation defined the word *rogue,* especially with anyone under the age of forty-five but in the older community his standing could be describe as *immaculate*.

He knew how to manipulate the uneducated. He knew how to alter times, places and suspects with tactical words and questions. He was that black cop that fucked with black boys just because he could. He knew that their lack of intelligence was a tool of his advantage.

They couldn't see the trap he laid for them. He was the deadly spider in the hole waiting for you to send vibrations down the line. The corners of the city all were extensions of his spiral silk web.

He'd drive by and watch you sell dope on the block on Monday and do nothing, then, turn around and arrest you on Friday for doing the same thing he acknowledged days before. He was evil-intelligent that way. He understood the psychology of an ignorant black adolescent standing on the bend of the street. He was great at mental warfare-they trained him well in the academy. They must have had to have a course on how to trick young black males in the academy. He confused them, kept them on their toes that dangled on the edge of a cliff.

Jameson had two faces ‘protect and serve’ cop on one side, and “get the fuck off the corner” cop on the other. Me, personally, I think he is crooked, but I couldn’t prove it, but the streets would agree with me if I ever took a survey.

In the community, he shined. He knew who to talk too, who to shake hands with, and who to break bread with and doing those things kept him in virtuous favor of the Mayor Saamiya Carter-Franklin, and Police Chief Bernard Ward. He patrolled the streets, he reassured the elderly that they were safe in one of the most notorious cities in America.

Romano, the driver, always had a frowned up look on his face, he was short and muscular with jet-black kinky hair and. He wore his pride in ink with detailed tattooed images of Italian flags on his forearms that he made sure were visible with the tight short sleeve cop shirts he wore.

My uncle never trusted white cops; they reminded him of the dudes he was with in the army. Most of them he said went from the Army, to the police force, which is cool, only problem though, they came to our neighborhoods with all that hard-ass white-boy shit. Joey Romano was that type. Tried his best to talk like we do, walk like we do, but all that shit he does, is just him mocking us, because I know he don’t take that shit home to his wife and kids.

It was shameful to watch Jameson stand there as his partner disrespected our culture and mannerisms. Acting like he was in a blackface minstrel show but on a corner under streets lights instead of a stage. Jameson was the opposite depending on who he was in front of at the time. He was one of ours but if he could bleach his skin or magically turn white to fit the occasion he would do it in a heartbeat. I watched him one time tighten up is butt-checks and get all proper around a white board member who was walking into the school.

Together they made a lethal combination and that was all we needed around here-two more ways to end up dead.

Anger begins in folly, and ends in repentance.

-Pythagoras

7

FOLLY

JAMESNON CHANTED LIKE a sarcastic announcer in a press box when he saw me. He laid out his punk-ass fist for me to give him a knuckle-bump-dap. I flicked the back of my hand against his.

"The four-the three-the two-touchdown by Walter Jameson Jr. and the crowd goes crazy."

I don't let myself get caught up in Jameson's daily folly.

fol-ly /fale/: lack of good sense; foolishness.

"Coach-man, give my boy the rock, thirteen carries ain't enough," Jameson said sitting on the edge of his desk.

His son wouldn't even be playing if Yosef were still alive. I'm thinking.

"We got a few kids who need carries; receptions, whatever… but I hear you?" I said.

"Nah-Ant, ya'll do a good job out there"-standing with his arms crossed- "just saying."

"I know exactly what you're just-saying, you want your son to get all carries."

"Nah-COACH, what I'm saying is, that you would give the ball to Yosef twenty times a game, and now my boy gets ten, or eleven carries and that's weak because he way better than that and ya'll know it."

"Well let's not talk about Yosef, he ain't got anything to do with this, and who is yall-you always had a pronoun problem? I'm the one who calls the plays and like I told you before Walt, I call what is open from the scouting report and what's working as the game plays out- man you played, so you know exactly what I mean, each game is different and you know that shit."

"Ease up Ant, I do know the game and I know my son can help yall more than he is right now, and as far as Yosef goes, I loved him too, he was good cat, but he got caught up with the wrong crowd, especially when he started fuckin-around with Isum Duart. See, if he don't associate himself with a dude like that-things might be different for both of them. Yosef would still be alive and Isum punk-ass wouldn't be locked up."

"Yeah, maybe, maybe not," I said irritated by his words.

"Still though, I tried to save Yosef, regardless of anything else. Shit so fucked up it's one thing if a kid gets shot or whatever like that-but another thing when you talking find a teenager dead under some bleachers, with no sign of foul play.

"Yeah, I don't get that either, been on my mind for a year now, it's just sad… sad that he is gone and that we don't really know why or how, and just sad that… my class about to start I gotta roll."

Jameson, not letting me walk away without getting in the last word. "I said back then, and still say, that he had to hit his head on the way down on a beam. Those bleachers ain't high enough to kill you from a fall. I-I don't know. I been on the force for a while and never seen, or ever heard, no shit like what happened to him-just falling off some bleachers, okay Ant', good luck on Friday, you know I will be there," he said as I walked away.

"Yeah I know, because I always hear that big ass mouth," I said in a mumble.

He must think that I am dumb or don't listen to good. He said that 'maybe Yosef would still be alive if he didn't run with Isum…does that mean that Isum mighta killed Yosef...or that Jameson knows more than what he is telling me about what really went down that night?

At the other end of the hallway was John Browbow the Principal and Head Food Football Coach. Browbow was a big dark skinned man that stood six-three and two hundred fifty pounds. He graduated from Franklin Smith University then moved to Youngstown nineteen years ago from Baltimore. He was an all-state offensive tackle in high school and followed that same effort at Franklin Smith University-had a pro tryout too.

Browbow still had some resemblance of his younger physique mainly in the shoulders and neck, it was his belly that revealed that his former self was long gone. He kept strict rules, he understood the type of kids he was dealing with, he didn't like the hallways cluttered with bodies that were late to class and that was his main goal each morning to make sure that they were in their proper place, a classroom.

Browbow and I had grown close over the years. He trusted me and made me Associate Head Coach. He gave me my first coaching job fresh out of college and much responsibility along with it. He put me in charge of student-athlete academics and community service outreach, along with being the offensive coordinator. I was young and had the energy to do all three of those jobs with ease.

I respected him and his position he held. He did a lot for the students.

His wife, Deirdre was the schools most popular teacher and his daughter Marva was not too far behind one of the most in popular students in the junior class. She was a cheerleader and a 4.0 student. The Browbows' were a family affair at Southside.

"We putting in that play today coach?' I asked.

"If we have time, we got a lot to cover today, Rayen has a good defense and we have to make sure we show all of their defensive fronts, and you got to get them fat-tail lineman moving man, they sho-nuff slow us down."

"Okay Coach, gotta get to first period, if I'm late, you going to have to write me a pass," I said laughing.

I stimulate life, and matter in my circumference.
None could ever match my palm, I'm calm
So you know when I blow the bomb.
It's gonna quake something like a migraine pain
It's gonna ache something-stopping all motion
You could never move against the energy intensity knowledge my reality
Everything flow mathematically in order
My universal gravity pull is magnetic.

- Masta Killa

8

YO

BEFORE MY CLASS fills up, I sit in silence trying to capture one more supplicating moment.

In the bottom right drawer of my desk, I keep my grandmother's Bible in a plastic bag. It's the same Bible that she gave to my uncle the day he boarded that bus headed to boot camp.

The pages were brittle and falling apart and each time I opened it, more pieces broke off. I kept it in the plastic bag for that reason. This Bible is sacred to me. I study from it, turning each page softly to read precept after precept, picking up the true lessons of the book.

Antietam Anthony Jones is my full name. I am the boy who made good from his neighborhood. I consider myself a soldier of misfortune, fighting one common cause, and that is not to fall-off and let these kids end up in coffins before their time.

I take pride in being a ghetto-scholar, teaching life and how to be a-first-fruit of God. This book, that many of us hate, saved my life. I speak about it every day and try to the best of my ability to live the laws, statutes and commandments but at times, I fall short. I know who is in the book, the true carriers of the heritage of Abraham, Isaac and Jacob, the seed of David. These are the lessons that my uncle blessed me with that I cherished and practice, morning, noon, and night…well, at least until Yosef died, that's when I started to backslide.

The students showed up to my class even if they skipped others. I love them and they love me back, they know being in here, learning would happen, not all book learning, but life learning that related to things they could actually use outside the school on the street.

I graduated from Southside seventeen years ago. I was just like the boys in my class and that I coach, young, black, and full of all this entelechy. It's my turn to give back to them what was given to me. This school was different in 1989, different than it was when my uncle or Brinson went here, neighborhood too. There were only a handful of white students during my time but by my ninth grade year, they had all left for the outer ring schools, so Southside High within a short time became all black, a-hood-school, as the kids call it now.

The only white faces around here are the older white teachers-sprinkled in with the younger rookies fresh out college. Only four black staff members worked in the building-Coach Browbow and his wife, the custodian Mr. Hall, and me. I wish it were more of us, but it's not, not sure why, but that's how it is around here. Maybe, I thought, that educated blacks were just so happy to have an education that they don't want to share it. But you know what, I also wondered why Coach Browbow, being a black Principal, didn't hire or try to find more black teachers to employ here or maybe he did.

Anyway, I have the chance to make a difference and that is my main goal when I walk through these doors each day. Books, movies, whatever it takes to gain their attention I use it. I know that our kids are "at-risk", because I was once at-risk, but I wasn't at risk of being locked in a game of black-jeopardy, or a game of black-rock-paper-scissors, shoot or be shot, or staying poor, ending up in jail or worse-DEAD.

I got my lesson together for my first period class. We were at the end of reading the novel *Native Son* by Richard Wright. I had promised the class that if we read every chapter aloud and made it to the end of the book, then we would watch the movie adaptation.

The looks on their faces and the closed novels that sat on each desk told me that they were aware that today was movie day and although this was a class of the toughest kids to teach, their childlike excitement came forth, glowing, like new copper pennies.

"As I promised today we will start watching the movie *Native Son*. I need everyone to pay attention, don't be on your phone, don't daydream, don't have your heads down and please no talking. If you play close attention you will recognize one of the characters in this movie.

"Who?" Asked Melvin Gregory.

"Yo-mamma," cracked Darnel as the class busted out in laughter.

I laughed in my mind.

"Take it easy fellas; listen up…so before I turn on the movie, let's sum up what we have read to make sure we are all on the same page of understanding exactly what is taking place in the novel."

Surprisingly, several hands pushed up in the air. An instant satisfaction warmed my body.

"Funch, what have you gotten from the novel so far?"

"He was a poor black boy who lived with his mother and brother and sister. He liked to rob people to make money…he acts just like some of these dumb boys round here act. Somebody always getting robbed out here," she said.

"True-but why is that?" I asked.

Hands shot up again, fewer than before.

"Calvin, let's hear your what you think."

"Well, I think the main character is desperate, he gotta feed his family and sometimes you gotta do bad stuff to take care of yo-peoples. Man, people don't really be understanding how hard it be out here."

The class began to bustle with side conversations of acknowledgment of what Calvin said. I seized the opportunity to tie Funchs's and Calvin's comment into one.

"Remember it's the 1930's on the South Side of Chicago. The main character, Bigger Thomas, is poor, uneducated, twenty-year-old black man who lives in a small apartment with his family. See, that rat in chapter one that he killed with that pan is important to the story. Hold on, before any of you even ask me why a rat is important to a story, let me finish explaining."

A sudden quietness swept over the room and all eyes were on me.

"That rat…represents Biggers daily struggle of having grown up under the climate of racial prejudice in 1930s America. That rat is just a metaphor of poverty and even though he killed it, it didn't change his circumstances. You just can't kill away being poor and uneducated. Bigger is stuck with the fact that he has no control over his life and that he cannot aspire to anything other than some menial low paying job.

His mother makes him to take a job with a rich white man named-Mr. Dalton, but Bigger instead would rather hook up with his friends to plan the robbery of a white owned store.

Bigger's everyday life is a life with all the wrong adjectives: anger, fear, and frustration. He is forced to hide behind a fake toughness or risk being carved up by the streets.

Bigger sees white people as an oppressive monster that follows him around every day. Bigger, like many black men, back then and today, are afraid to confront this monster and we let it overwhelm us, but rather than admit he is afraid, he backs out of the robbery by starting a fight with his firend."

"That's why he did that?" asked Kavion.

"Yes, he had to do something to make up a reason not do the robbery. It's sorta like for the same reasons we find excuses to kill each other. We make up different reasons because of our fear and our oppression is driving us insane, so we take it out on one another, it's what the media calls black on black crime. Somewhere along our journey in this country we were taught to hate each other and we express that hate through physical violence and destruction of the places where were live and go to school.

Bigger was no different. Just because it was 1930 does not mean things were different; it was just a different year but same people.

Listen, Bigger kept falling and falling mentally until his mind got so twisted that he saw no way out other than to kill a person. That family, the Daltons-the father owned the apartment building that Bigger and his family lived in, so when he found that out and had to deal with the way Mr. Dalton treated him and spoke to him, he snapped. The daughter just happened to be a casualty of a man gone insane with anger."

"But he didn't have smoother her and then burn her body," Jasmin Clackson said in a sensitive hurt voice.

"I agree, but think about the panic that was going through his mind at that moment. You have to realize that in 1930, a black man kills a white woman, accident or not, it's the electric chair. Bigger didn't have money to get the proper legal counsel to prove that it was an accident, so he was doomed the moment he put his hands on her and carried her up those stairs. The kissing part is irrelevant by that point, although that was a death sentence as well.

He should of left Mary Dalton in that car, went, and told her parents to get her. He forgot his place in society, his place as a black man who was poor and uneducated like that rat. He would have remained invisible to Mr. Dalton if he would have stayed under that stove but he scurried, and got smashed by a pan."

"Metaphor-right-Coach Jones?" asked Calvin.

"Sure is, but you tell me what I meant by that metaphor."

"Bet-I see it like this, like in rap music, when they use metaphors about money, you know, like cheese, dough, bread, G, this dude Bigger killed that rat cause the rat came out in the open. The rat obviously been living there for a while, so if he woulda just kept living like he was invisible then he could still be eating cheese. Bigger shoulda just been cool with driving the Dalton family around, stack up his bread and try and move his family out the projects."

Calvin sat back in his chair proudly.

"Yes-sir Calvin…what you said is right and exact. Bigger Thomas is us, me and you, this city, the people that you see each day as you walk home from school.

The Author, Richard Wright writes in such a way that he makes you enter Bigger's mind through words. Those words try to give you an understanding of the devastating effects of the social conditions in which Bigger was raised. Bigger was not born a violent criminal. He wasn't a little kid and said to himself "one day ima kill a person." He is a product of American culture and the violence and racism that saturate it. He is a "native son." A son of his conditions like we all are…

"Jones," a kid yells out my last name.

"First of all, that's Mr. Jones or Coach Jones, we not friends or the same age, so try it again."

"My fault-Jones…I mean Coach. This dudes name was really Bigger-why would his moms name him Bigger?" LaMarcus asked.

See how these kids test you. Then they wonder why they struggle in life. I clearly corrected him about addressing me the right way, but he still had to show his peers that he can't or won't follow any directions. I really don't want to even answer him, but I did anyway.

"Yes, his name is Bigger, LaMarcus probably for the same reason your name is LaMarcus-because that is what your parents decided to name you…go turn off the lights."

I connected the projector to my computer and started the DVD. The students silenced themselves and watched attentively. I sat down and my mind went directly to football. I take coaching seriously. I put in the work for us to be the best. I try to coach the game the right way.

We need to attack the outside of their defense. I thought to myself.

I need to break down every strategy, every scenario, of what we can do and what we can't do, that's called X's and O's in coaching language.

I wish we had Yosef, but he is dead.

The morning flew by me. I was looking forward to lunch because that was the time I could relax and watch film of who we are about to play. I eat alone in my room, with the door locked, the lights out, window shades down, all to send the message of not to be disturbed.

Every day as I sit in this room, in this chair, alone, he comes to me in a prayer for the dying. Yosef, was five-ten and a hundred fifty-five pounds. He had a slim athletic build, with a peached fuzzed beard at the bottom of his face. He was comely. He had the face of a young movie star and the personality to match. The sound of his voice caused you to be at ease around him, his temper held its peace.

He was ranked as one of the best junior tailbacks in the state. I made him into a dynamic player from all those backyard games we shared years ago. Then, when he stepped on the field, it all came out in electrifying fashion. He was a playmaker and the whole city loved to see him shine under the Friday night lights.

Yosef grew up down-the-hill on Falls Avenue with his grandparents Hershel and Mildred Nassy. Old people, with old values, and beliefs raised him and that didn't always sit well with his youth. Those were the days when I would step in and let him crash at my house only to hammer into him, about "honoring thy mother and father."

Yosef loved to be social and spent a lot of his time in the streets, not selling drugs or up to no good, he just like to be around people, he enjoyed them, but being a hood-socialite came with its own set of issues and problems. Popularity in the streets of Youngstown sometimes worked in his favor, but most of the time it did not.

There was always somebody challenging him, trying to test his metal to see if it would dent or melt. Being “the man” at sports brings out a different kinda of jealousy on the block, it’s that “I wish I was you” type of envy that Yosef had to face out there. The same way I did when I was his age, which is the real problem between Jameson and me today.

Yosef knew how to protect himself, that was not my real concern but my task was to get him to use his brains, plus football, to get out of what the national media called, “Murder Town USA.”

Yosef was a good student, who was not afraid to let people around him know that he took learning serious. He attended all of his classes on time and sat no further back than the second row. All of his teachers liked him and made sure he kept up with his work. Yosef didn’t slack, he didn’t cheat his way to where he had gotten so far. He would have been one more in a long line of Southside players to go on to the next level. He was that good. As good as Yosef was, he was the third best player on our team behind All-American quarterback- Hutch ‘Hue’ Campbell, and Isum Duart, an All-State defensive end-who on the street, was-known as, Poop-pa-doo.

Despite all of that about him, the purest thing was his humbleness and respect he had for girls. Don’t get me wrong, he liked girls and they liked him back, but he didn’t use his status to gain access to the hearts of women.

He had a love interest in Coach Browbow’s daughter Marva and he used to talk of marrying her after college, even though Isum used to tell him he was crazy for even thinking her parents would let that happen, but he still spoke it into life.

The Browbow’s approved of Yosef dating their daughter, well so it appeared. Yosef treated her with respect and never tried to get out of line with his actions or behavior towards her. Mrs. Browbow cared for Yosef like a son she never had, and always made sure that he was eating on a regular basis probably because she felt sorry for him like he didn't get fed enough at home.

Marva L. Browbow was one of the top students at Southside. It wasn't a fact but more like a general speculation that his academic success was only because of who her parents were, but I never believed that about her. Marva had a driven personality and I think, even if she grew up in the projects, she would still be intelligent and achieve the things she did. Much like Yosef, or Hutch, she was a victim of girls' resentment and other unfavorable behaviors from her peers.

Marva had the young appearance of what I imagined her mother looked like at that age. Her face was soft and warm with innocence. Caring was in her eyes and her smile radiated like the sun. Her arms stayed filled with books that she carried neatly as if they were glued together. Her parents didn't dote on her at school, they treated here the same as any other student.

Marva had a few friends who stayed locked to her hip, one, being a girl named Raquel Boyd and the other, Lauren Billings, both who Marva had known since elementary.

Raquel was small, petite you could say. She had a soft but structured face. Her dress was conservative, but fly enough to be in-line with the latest fashions. She was the lead writer of the schools newsletter and that kept her in the loop of all gossip and business that floated around the schoolhouse. She had gained citywide writers rank when she wrote an article about Yosef's death and a possible police cover up. When those words hit the hallways and lunch tables, it caused a stir downtown and rumor had it that the Mayor called the school board to have her silenced.

Rachel loved Marva. She protected her from metaphoric darts thrown by girls who had diva-rank and were motivated to keep Marva in their imaginary place, beneath them. Marva was a target envy for having educated parents who worked in the school. That fact made daily school life hard for Marva, so Raquel along with Lauren made sure Marva stayed bullet proof.

I wrapped up the remainder of my lunch and began my rounds from class to class checking on the players making sure they were in attendance and earning passing grades. My first stop was always Mrs. Browbows science class where there were eight players on her roster.

I rolled up slowly and crept in the door as not to interrupt her lesson.

"The study of plants is called what?" She asked the class. "Plant Biology," several of them yelled out.

"Yes, now open your books to chaaaaapter… thirty-one, and begin reading silently, and we will go over the reading in about twenty minutes."

After directing her class to work, Mrs. B came over to me.

"Hey Coach, how are you, I know this is a tough week for you, but be blessed and encouraged-its homecoming."

"Yes, I'm okay for the most part, trying to hold tight to my emotions. I miss him."

I said.

"Yeah, and we do too, I'm trying to hold Marva together as well, the closer we get to Friday the more I worry about her, but I'm so glad that wild child Raquel has been here to help me out with her, she's crazy but she is a good friend. Big Browbow seems to be doing okay though, you know he is the strong don't show emotion type of man."

"After practice I'm going up to see Isum, we can't forget about him," I said.

"No we can't, I'm glad you visit him, he needs a positive person in his life, Lord knows he doesn't have it anywhere else."

Try to let you know
Just want to let you see
The real is all I know
Real is what I be
Time is now for y'all
Now is now for me
Life is beautiful
This the story of me

- Masta Ace

9

MONDAY: DAT'S WHAT"S HAPPENIN'

IT'S MONDAY AFTER PRACTICE…

Isum was locked-up at the Juvenile Justice Center on the lower West Side of town. The juvies called the facility the Happening House, because some shit was always happening up in there.

Isum Duart was locked up because he had too much Bigger Thomas in his blood. This wasn't his first time behind oxidized steel bars but I prayed that this would be his last.

Isum was the son of Ibraheem Duart, one of the best shoulda-been-coulda-been athletes in Youngstown. No, it wasn't the drug game that defeated Ibraheem, it was the fear of success that scared him away from taking that scholarship to college and that left him as a wonderer back and forth from Youngstown to Cleveland. Now his son sows the seed of abandonment.

People on the street said that Isum was the reason that Yosef was dead, which makes me think back to my conversation with Jameson, but in the police file, Isum was charged with carrying a loaded gun, firing it in a school safety zone, felonious assault and resisting arrest.

I looked up the law for a case like Isum's on Google and in a felony-case, after the arraignment, if the case does not settle or get dismissed then the judge holds a preliminary hearing. At this hearing, the judge will decide if there is enough evidence that the defendant committed the crime to make the defendant have to appear for a trial. If the judge decides that there is enough evidence, the prosecutor will file a document called "the Information." Then, the defendant will be arraigned, a second time, on the information. At that time, the defendant will enter a plea and proceed to trial. I had to read this a few times for it to make any sense. What I came up with was that Isum was in some shit, especially since he would have to face Prosecutor Dominic Stanley and he had a history of batting a thousand when it came to locking up black juveniles.

I walked into the visitors' meeting room at the Happening House. This is a small usually quiet spot for the visitors that the inmates put on their visitors list. The room was filled with decent sitting furniture and sufficient lighting for reading birthday cards or mailed letters from friends. It was crowded with three races of people, mostly black and Hispanic and a few white.

Isum came around the corner. I could see his face behind the thick glass window of the heavy security door. A buzzer sounded and Isum and a guard walked directly over to where I was sitting.

He sat down.

I started right in on him, barely giving him the chance to get comfortable in his chair.

"I didn't always do right Isum, I wasn't always in the truth, even now I am struggling with living and doing the right things. I asked the Most High-what am I supposed to do with all the temptations that face me each day.

Isum, you see the streets didn't want to let me go, the streets grip is tighter than any grip you will ever know or experience, there are things that happened to me back when I was your age that I still think about-things that happen to me in those same streets outside this door. Things that I still have nightmares about and to keep it real-still get scared about those things that happened in my past.

The Devil knew I was trying to get out of his game, because every night that I prayed- I snitched on him. I hoped and prayed to get past those bad days-to be able to out run the Devil like I outran defenders on the football field.

I tried drinking all types of different alcohol trying to hide in a bottle of poison, still thinking I would be okay, because I was young, and I thought I had time- but I really didn't have time and you don't either.

Down inside my heart I was somebody else and I had a love inside me that I wouldn't let anybody ever see- until Yosef came, then I matured, and saw what I needed to do for him. I chased the Devil away from me- away from Yosef, but each day and night he came back and again I chased him away. And from Yosef came you and the other players, all of you God brought into my life for a reason Isum.

I started to know who I was according to God… not no religion- not no Muslim-not no Baptist-not none of that… and that is why Satan keeps coming back after me, because he knows that I know who I really am and you too."

As I spoke, I could see other young men around us begin to listen. They overheard me because I spoke loudly on purpose, to share this message with all these young black misguided minds that walked to and fro' like sleepwalkers.

"I saw a lot of dudes die, my boy-Little Donnie he was one of my best childhood friends, and he is gone. Shot dead on the end of my block over what- a few crack rocks. I loved him too and if I had a brother, I woulda wanted it to be him. I see his moms around and her face ain't the same since he been gone.

I watched my friends get consumed with fire because they stayed drunk and high while I was fighting to stay in the truth that I was taught and they survived by the grace of God. I was almost like these so-called tough dudes up in here. Then I wised up, changed my mind, changed my friends, and started applying my uncle's teachings. I dodged the long ride that Yosef had to take by the same grace of God.

I have traveled and been to a-lot of places, but ain't no place like home Isum. I kiss my finger and cross my heart praying to make it out these dark days…I miss Donnie his death hurts. I promised him, as he laid there dead in that casket, that I would live for him and me. I envision the days we had together as his voice whispers in my mind telling me to stay focused. He was me once upon a time."

Isum acted as if he wasn't listening to me but I could tell he was, he leaned on my words that I spoke to him, but still trying to maintain his hardness in front of the other boys.

"The book of Matthew says and I quote, *he that hath ears to hear, let him hear…*"

That annoyed him, whenever I quoted the book.

"Man-Coach, here you go with this again," Isum said.

"Yeah, you right, here I go with it again, the truth is, not everybody gon make it on the last day Isum, most of your partna's gon die, because dey black ass demons and right now, you on that demon shit right with them. Yeah, here I go again…praying for you all the time, here I go again coming here to see you, when I don't have too, yeah here I go again trying to help tough ass Isum Duart. Yeah, you right, here I go again waiting for young black men like you to wake the hell up and see what is really going on around here. When you get out of here-this cage, don't go back…"

"Back to what-being locked up, this my last time up in here man," Isum said.

"Good, but I'm not talking about coming back here Isum, don't go back to your vomit. Think about what I just said and I will see you Thursday," and I left him sitting at the table.

I walked outside and stood at the top of the chipped cement steps. "Here I go again" I said out loud.

Bodies funneled past me. Anxious faced visitors ran up the stairs all jockeying to get in line. Bright eyed little kids, pants sagging teenagers who seemed to be all dressed the same moving in step like it was an amusement park they were about to enter.

I sat down on the top stair thinking of nothing in particular. I was tired of thinking about shit. It was wearing me down the ghosts that haunt my mind. They were winning and I was losing, no matter how hard I fought them off, I was still losing. Here I am telling Isum to fight the Devil off and look at me, losing to him right now. I wear a mask to hide my pain, I wear a mask to disguise who I really am, my face on the outside seems normal, but it's really an ugly twisted mask.

I sat there for a few more minutes, then Donnie's face manifested in my head. I could vividly see his eyes looking into mine. I thought about him standing next to me on that starting line, his foot even with my own. His smile bright and clean as we waited for those races to start. Then suddenly we grew apart, for no other reason than life getting in our way and as we grew older, I saw less and less of him. I don't speak about Donnie to anyone outside of myself and only down in the basement when I sit in the dark.

I reached in my pocket and pulled out a pen. I wrote this on the back of a paper receipt I found in a half-dead flowerbed next to me. ‘Ghetto living is parallel to prison.

For all humanity and soul's heavy
Ride thru life like an old Chevy
Look at the world thru your rearview,
and honk your horn till they hear you
So after you're gone its tribute.

- Killah Priest

10

THE HARDEST DAY

A YEAR AGO, the morning of Yosef's funeral, hundreds of people slowly filed into the Morning Star Baptist Church on the lower Eastside to mourn the loss of this young man.

The Morning Star was a staple in the community. This was my first time here and it was beautiful inside and out. You could see the new renovations all around. The architect had enough vision to keep the old stain glass windows which gave off a rich color palette of light-matching the old with the new. Tall white pillars stood strong on the outer edge of the sanctuary. The baptismal pool sat high above the preachers chair like a crown of clear water above his head. Big box speakers were suspended from tightened brackets in all four corners of the large octagon room. Cushioned maroon bench pews created a comfortable resting place for hours of preaching that I'm sure happened in here every Sunday. Every bench had a new bible and hymn book resting in a wooden book ledge that was screwed into its back.

The Pastor, Kenneth Donaldson would eulogize Yosef. He was a longtime friend of mine from youth football. He had just moved back to Youngstown from Tennessee to take over the church. He was dressed in a priestly purple robe and sat front and center flanked by his assistants. I informed Mr. Nassy that I would handle all the arraignments with Pastor Donaldson and Coach Browbow put up three thousand dollars of his own money to help to pay expenses.

Ushers were dressed in black with solemn faces directing each mourner down to their seat handing each of them an obituary. The pews filled up quickly, some of the people not evening knowing Yosef, but pinched their way in to show their respects to this fallen football player.

Coaches from across the city brought their players dressed in their game jerseys to show love and support of what had become one of the saddest days in the history of this city.

An open section was blocked-off for our team and coaching staff who rode two school buses to the church. The Nassy family sat up in front directly across from the open casket of their deceased Grandson. His Chicago grandparents sat behind them. Next to them, I sat with Adrienne hand in hand and the team behind us.

To my right there were other family members of Yosef's who I guess were from out of town, some older and some younger, dressed flamboyantly and simple. I didn't recognize any of them which made me wonder how close Yosef was to his extended family and actually how alone he really was here in his short time on earth.

I became dejected deep down inside over the lamentation of abandonment, but being rescued, but still left abandoned nonetheless. The fact of having someone to care for you, but that care coming out of force and not request, having to make a real family out of kids on a team or friends on a coaching staff. I looked at Yosef-dead-alone in that casket having had to live a put-together puzzle life with no real family or at least family he never really got to know.

***

Yosef was neatly dressed in a soft colored black suit with a red bow tie and a gold-plated warrior head pinned to his left lapel. Across his chest lay his crisply folded jersey and a hand painted football signed by each player that Hutch presented to Mr. Nassy. His coffin was surrounded by flowered arrangements, flanked by two large picture easels, one, holding an action photo of him celebrating in the end zone and the other a polished mahogany framed number twenty-seven jersey that would be hung in the hallway of the school.

On each side of the casket stood two assistant coaches, the proud centurions tasked with the job of keeping control of emotional grievers who passed by the body.

The time had come for the invocation by Pastor Donaldson, followed by the reading of two scriptures,

2 Corinthians 4: 16-18 and 1 Samuel 1: 27-28.

The Southside High Choir was up next singing a musical selection- Someday We'll All Be Free. Offensive Guard Jose' Palomino sang the lead part and had the whole church in tears.

The time had come for family members and friends to speak about Yosef. The ushers directed people to the outer walls of the sanctuary forming a line in front of the two microphone stands. There were so many who wanted to speak that the Pastor had to limit the number of people allowed to get in line and limit each to two-minutes. Many of Yosef's peers used this time to overly express their deep friendship they had with him, one trying to out-do the other. The respectful ones who followed directions used that time to-just-say goodbye. All of those speeches whether long or short added to my tenseness, because I was the one asked to precede the pastor's eulogy.

"You okay?" Adrienne whispered in my ear. My head dropped. "Yeah I'm cool for the most part, not sure what to say, I thought I would-I had it all together all week in my head but now…"

"Well you have to pay your respects and they asked you to speak about him because who better to do it then you?" She asked. "Just speak from your heart, you knew him better than anyone here other than his grandparents, so just speak of how you knew and loved him."

"No doubt, no doubt," I said as I gazed at the obituary page with my name it.

My anxiety began to get the best of me. I am usually cool under pressure but this time wasn't. I began to pray… **"**God, I'm asking for your help. I know that I can't change anything that you put into motion… I am asking you to let me speak without falling over my words-that the things that I'm about to say be honest and true. I know how I feel inside and that what I feel may come out with clarity… but since we are all here, all in pain and mourning, I am asking for your blessing for all of these people who loved Yosef Nassy… he was a good kid, he was trying."

My legs feel like weights and I can feel the heat of pressure coming over me, Adrienne nudged me to get up, it was time. I edged to the end of my seat and my mind continued in prayer. "God this is hard for me, because that could have been me dead years ago. Up until now God you have spared me. I don't understand how all this happened. I'm not ready to die, don't call me yet. I got too much stuff to do.

Jesus… my hands aren't clean in this I could have did more for him and Isum."

I stood up, holding Adrienne's fingertips, letting our grasp softly break. I approached Yosef's dead body, climbing to the top of the podium that towered above and as I stood over him, my mind flashed back in an instant, to all those years to when I first saw his face.

I took a deep breath deeper than I had every taken and then I lifted my eyes from him and faced the crowd. I could see all the young innocent eyes of all the players looking up at me, many of them with teared streaked faces, some with heads down and some looking afraid to move. I adjusted the microphone, cleared the fear from my throat and began to speak.

"First, I want to offer my condolences to Yosef's grandparents and the rest of his family. My name is Antietam Jones and I was Yosef's mentor and one of his coaches. I wanted to say to everyone here, that Yosef was a good young man. I'm not saying that he was a good because that is what is always said at funerals about young people who pass away, but he really was a good kid- a kid who had a restless heart, and was always ready to-go-to-move-to-dream and he made his share of mistakes, but always tried to either fix them or not repeat them.

I met Yosef in 1997 when he was nine years old. I was volunteering at the Boys Club, which if you don't know is on the Southside of town on Oakhill Avenue.

He was leaning up against a brick wall outside. He was just there leaning…the same way he leaned on the fence at practice or in the hallway in school. If you knew him, then you know that lean that he would do. He was posing with his arms folded like all of a sudden a photographer was gonna run up and take his picture. He was with a few other boys that I had seen from time to time and to be honest, a few of them were little knuckleheads but had older brothers who were real troublemakers. I decided from that moment to steal Yosef away from them. I don't know my reasons for taking a liking to him at the time, he said no words to me, or made any gesture that he needed saving, but that little boy would become more to me that I ever imagined.

His grandparents, Mr. and Mrs. Nassy, raised him and I was raised by my uncle, both of us were born, swaddled, and just handed-over, me to a Vietnam Veteran and him, to his grandparents who sit in front of me today.

We would spend hours together and during those hours, I would try my best to keep him focused on the right things. He was under attack from the evils of society. He was under attack by his so-called friends who would rather see him hanging out instead of being with me. Years had gone by and I watched him grow into a young man who had a bright future. By this time he had not only become like a little brother to me, he also became a fixture at my house. He stayed with me from time to time, which I welcomed because he was all I really had to love at that point in my life. Eight years is not a lot of time to know someone but I am glad that he and I had that time to be together.

Before I close, I would be wrong not to mention my uncle. My uncle Kay-kee Smith died years ago but his spirit lives within my own. My uncle served in the Vietnam War and that experience hardened him to fear, so much so, that he once saved a little boy from a burning house. People who witnessed it said he ran into that house before the firefighters had a chance too. He was that type of man.

My uncle died years later in his sleep, not having to fight the demons from the war any longer, no longer having to fight the hurt he felt about my mother-his sister.

My memories of him are the best memories I have stored in my mind and right next to his, are the memories I have of Yosef…The day we buried my uncle I had thought I had lost my whole world, but I didn't, I gained a new world of my manhood. I remember being extremely hurt that he was gone forever. It was a grief that I thought I would never feel again well, I was wrong.

And if I can tell all the young people in this church today one thing, I will say… we need more 'good kids' because we sure enough have too many bad one's here in this city. It's okay to be a good black kid, you have one standing here before you, I'm from here, Pastor Donaldson is from here, we both were good black kids- and yes we made our mistakes but like I said we fixed them and did not repeat them. So before I sit down, I wanted to say to Yosef, that I love you and that I will never forget what you brought into my life... thank you."

I stood frozen for a second as the crowd applauded and shouted "Amen." I went back to sit down trying to subdue the tears I felt that bubbled up in my eyes. I continued to look upon the young face of Gods fallen Warrior. Adrienne squeezed my palm and I could feel her warmth and compassion and I knew that she was there for me to lean on.

The funeral was coming to its end. All of our faces tightened with fear of this being near to the close.

Pastor Donaldson began his eulogy of Yosef. He spoke of Yosef's meek nature, not the meekness of being weak or shy, but the true definition of the word-humble, strong and kind. He talked about the clubs that Yosef was involved in at school, clubs like drama and the book club. He spoke of how Yosef loved his teammates and coaches.

He spoke of all the true things about Yosef- true things, not the lies that some pastors tell about dead black kids knowing that they may have been involved in a young life of crime, that was feel good preaching according to Pastor Donaldson and he didn't do that. Now he didn't bad-mouth the dead, but he didn't glorify their evil lifestyle to save feelings or emotions. He was a master at getting his point across, but this one was easy…Yosef was a good kid so his eulogy flowed like water.

He made sure to mention that Yosef played little league football for the Hagstrom House Braves the same team that he and I played for in 1980.

Being a 'Brave' was important to the adult men across the city, being a "Brave" linked us together forever. "I remember those times like it was yesterday. The Braves… it's nice to think back, to hear and remember the best days in my life," I whispered to Adrienne.

"Are there any Braves in the church this morning, stand up for Yosef and let him know that you are here for him," Pastor proudly asked.

The people that stood pressed from wall to wall began to bustle around seeing who would stand, slowly men of all ages rose tall in representation of the formally named Willis Street Market Braves, The Hagstrom House Braves, Hillman Street Braves and New Bethel Braves.

I smiled as I looked around. I could see the players looking up at me. I closed my eyes and thought more about those days past. My mind fell back deep into Yosef's childhood, it made me smile.

The Pastor gave his closing remarks.

"Let us commend our brother Yosef Lamont Nassy to the mercy of God, our maker and redeemer, into your hands. O merciful Savior, we commend your servant Yosef. Acknowledge, we humbly beseech you, a sheep of your own fold, a lamb of your own flock, a sinner of your own redeeming."

***

The funeral directors slowly closed the casket. Yosef faded away into the blackness. No sooner had the locks been sealed, sounds of eerie moans wailed out into the air, a cry, at first muffled and broken, it was sound of children sobbing. The screams that swelled into the air blinded my eyes from the pierce-ness of the pitch. The coldness of closure crept its way around the church possessing the people into a hypnotic trance of sadness.

I stood up and felt myself stagger from the anguish of all the noise. Adrienne stood with me as she pressed her inner forearm into my lower back. My stomach started to churn and I began to feel faint. She sat me back down and fanned my face pushing the beads of sweat back towards my ears. Minutes passed and I regained myself.

Big Browbow commanded the team to stand and make a tunnel down the center isle of the church. The assistant pastor stood before the crowd and asked for six pallbearers, so me, Hutch Campbell, Jerome Jones, Coach Williams, Walter Jameson Jr. and Wendell Stewart grabbed Yosef's casket and slowly rolled it down the carpeted isle as the players set like tin soldiers in a row. The casket was heavy and I was nervous that I would trip, but I steadied my steps and focused my watery eyes. There was a polished black hearse waiting for him at the end of the stairs to take him to his final resting place.

The sun was shining holding back the brisk temperature and it seemed as if the entire city was there to say goodbye to Yosef Nassy-the Southside High Warrior. Each player gathered around the hearse holding hands and singing the schools fight song, many of them cried as they sang with manly pride for their collapsed friend.

"What do we do now coach?" I asked Big Browbow, as all the coaches' walked toward the parking lot away from the scattering crowd.

"We keep going. We keep practicing. We have a game tomorrow and we have to help these young men and make sure they know that we are here for them. This ain't unimaginable in their lives Anthony, look were they come from, look at this neighborhood, look at their chances… we have to provide them better chances, more hope, a real reality, not just in football but in everyday life."

***

Seven black cars aligned in the curved funeral driveway, each one slowly exiting out towards Tod Cemetery. Traffic stopped for miles adding to the agony of the final chapter in what was a maddening five days since his death. I wished the cars would move faster. I had a headache and had to fight back another anxiety attack that began crawling up my chest. I reached in my pocket and pulled out two Excedrin pills to solve my pain, which was another issue I have to live through. I began breathing slow, slowing down my fluttering heartbeat.

We pulled in creakingly slow into Tod, through the maze of winding roads passed dead loved ones of the City of Youngstown. The hearse stopped at plot 8, row S, grave #125. We carried Yosef's coffin over to the gravediggers assigned to consignment and the lowering of his body into the ground. Pastor Donaldson reopened his bible and read:

"Lord Jesus Christ, by your own three days in the tomb, you hallowed the graves of all who believe in you and so made the grave a sign of hope that promises resurrection even as it claims our mortal bodies. Grant that our brother Yosef Lamont Nassy, may sleep here in peace until you awaken him to glory, for you are the resurrection and the life. Then he will see you face to face and in your light will see the light and know the splendor of God, for you live and reign forever and ever. Amen."

That season we finished with a 6-4 record losing the last two games. It was an extremely cold fall and I was looking forward to the winter as to take a pause from all that had happened over the last few months.

***

The next Saturday me and Adrienne re-started our date-nights of dinner and a movie in hopes of trying to get tour lives back in order, our conversations about Yosef continued too.

"I'm glad football is over for a while," she said to me that night.

"Me too."

"It has been rough for you and all of us for that matter, but nowhere near as hard as it is for his grandparents," she said as she rubbed my hand affectionately as we whispered to each other before our steaks came out.

"Yeah you right," I said.

"What can we do to help them?" she asked.

"I went over there a few days after the funeral, Yosef's grandmother greeted me at the door and you could see the grief still pressed hard on her face. Mr. Nassy came out of a back room and came up to me and hugged me, he thanked me for all I had done for Yosef since he was a kid."

"That boy loved you," he said putting his hand on my shoulder.

"I loved him too sir…" I said back to him.

"What else did he say?" Adrienne asked.

"Not much more. He began pacing around over an oval carpet in the middle of the floor. He grabbed me by the arm and started leading me around his house. I had been in there before but you know I never really paid attention to all of the things that were around the room, all of Yosef's trophies from when he was little before I met him.

Mr. Nassy was actually one of Yosef's termite coaches, I saw it on a team picture, so he has been involved with his grandson and football his whole life. I waited for a moment, trying to gain my calmness from seeing Yosef as a child and a younger version of his grandfather; then I could feel my head starting to hurt from the grief from recalling that tender encounter. I reached deep into my pockets searching for things I already used. I asked him had they heard anything more from the police, Mrs. Nassy said that a Detective

Madison had closed the case and that Yosef died from the fall and that is what the final report will be."

Adrienne looked at me. "Don't you know Madison?"

"Sorta, I said."

Her eyes started to water, the tears meeting at her chin. I reached across the table and wiped her face.

"Babe listen, I know that was hard to hear," she said.

"The more I stood there, the more Mr. Nassy wanted to show. He took me to Yosef's room, he opened up a red trunk at the end of the bed and there was Yosef's last belongings from the night he died, folded up and placed neatly inside, along with his Hillman Street Braves jersey and that 1972- "*Luke Cage*" comic book that I gave him."

"Good ole' Luke Cage, I mumbled."

"I walked around his room and it reminded me of my own when I was his age. I guess times don't change much as we think. He reached down into the trunk and gave me Yosef's washed practice jersey and helmet. Yosef always carried his helmet around with him. His grandfather said they didn't need those things and that it was school property.

I thanked him and he walked me outside onto the porch, before I got to the bottom step, Mrs. Nassy stopped me and asked me to sit down on the swing with to her.

"What did she say," Adrienne asked.

"At first she just sat there with her eyes closed, she may have been praying, I didn't know for sure…then she looked up at me with a smile on her face."

She said, "Coach Jones, Yosef saw you as his father, we tried our best with him…he was never a problem, never talked-back to us…but he was raised by old people and all this computerized this-and-that didn't do me and his grandfather any good in Yosef's world.

To tell you the truth, we prayed to get him to the point we did. Then you came along, and you Coach, were the answer to our prayers. His grandfather didn't trust you at first, but I always knew that the Lord sent you to us."

"Her words made me puff up with pride. My ears wanted to hear more, but I never said anything to her, so I just sat there."

"Awww-baby," Adrienne sighed.

Adrienne was beautiful to say the least, educated, well rounded sista' from a better part of town and a better upbringing than I ever had. But she understood what kind of man I truly was and she was willing to help me fight the demons that were in my mind.

She was my safety net, I wanted to marry her but I didn't want to take that walk down the aisle with her until my mind and conscience was clear. I loved her no doubt; she represented two types of women that I so desperately craved in my life- caviar and fried chicken. There were times where she would be elegant, sophisticated and other times she could be street, tough- tough enough to stand toe to toe with me in a fight in an alley. She knew of my past, I made it a point never to lie to her because every man even the most messed up ones have to be able to live in some type of truth. She didn't judge me, she never questioned me, all she ever did was love me like no other woman had ever loved a man.

"Stop-it Adrienne, this ain't-no Hallmark moment."

"Then she started to tell me about Yosef's parents, both young she said. She said that both families got together and decided that they would all help raise Yosef, but that it didn't work out that way. She said it started off pretty good, but after a while Yosef just stayed with them and his other grandparents never tried to stop it…so he stayed with them full time, so me being prayed into his life was a blessing she said."

"Do you think it was a blessing Antietam?" Adrienne asked.

"Sometimes I do and sometimes I don't because what did I really do Adrienne, he is dead at 17 years old. I couldn't ever imagine being dead at that age."

"Me either."

"I got up, and went back down the steps and started walking to my car. Before I got in, Mr. Nassy stopped me. He came down to my truck door. He whispered and said that two cops came to the house after the funeral, one black and one white. I automatically assumed it was Jameson and Romano and I was right. Not that that is strange but…He said the black one immediately asked about Isum, like Isum was the one who was dead and not his grandson.

Mr. Nassy said, he told Jameson that he or his wife ain't didn't care about no other boy unless it had to do with Yosef's death.

"Jameson don't like that Isum boy at all," he said.

He looked around as if he were being watched. He leaned in closer and said that a boy walked by and threatened him not to talk to the police again. He said he was sitting on the steps and this boy walked up to him and basically threatened him. He said he told the boy to get out of his yard. The boy walked away the same way he came.

Then he just broke down and cried out, 'why couldn't my grandson just be hurt Coach, that's all I want to know is why? I even asked the Lord why, why is my grandson gone? Me and his grandmother trying our best to accept this…but the rest I just don't know.'

Mrs. Nassy came and gathered him and walked him back into the house. I ran back up to the door to see if he was okay. I looked through the screen and I could her walking him upstairs. I sat back down on the swing hoping that she would come back and tell me he was okay.

She never did. I called them a few hours later to check up on them.

He said he told Detective Madison and that Madison said he would look into it. Madison put cruisers on the block. The phone went quiet then. I could hear Mrs. Nassy in the background telling her husband to ask me…then he hit me with this…

"With what," Adrienne asked.

Here is a black elderly couple, retired, living their twilight in sadness over their only grandson who is no longer here. How hurt must they be Adrienne to offer me money to help them find answers they may never get and if they do, will it drive away the pain of being broken hearted."

"Money, the offered you money, to do what?"

"To find answers, answers that Madison and Jameson get paid to find, not me-an assistant football coach. Mr. Nassy said he would pay me five-thousand dollars to find out what happened to Yosef, five-thousand!"

"What did you say?"

"What do you think I said…I said no…but I promised him that I would do whatever I could to help them."

"Where you able to tell them anything?" Adrienne asked.

"Like what Adrienne? Yeah nothing but a bunch of I-don't-knows, I-wish-I-did-know, but I-just-don't-know, but I'm going to look into it even if the cops don't want to anymore. I know enough people downtown, uptown and on the shadiest backstreets.

Rumors are flying around like the bugs under my porch light, Yosef killed himself over a girl, Isum killed Yosef, Marva killed Yosef, some dudes from the Northside killed Yosef…it just goes on and on. Yosef was stronger than that, he may have fell by accident or have been murdered-but he didn't commit suicide-no way."

"I'm just asking that's all, but you spoke to Isum, what about him, what did he say?" she asked.

"Shit, what about him? At least he is still alive, I talked to him one-time, and that conversation was more about me, rather than what happened that night at the L.

Isum Duart lives two lives with two sets of friends Adrienne, one life of football and those friends, and the other life of the street and those friends; he sorta is serving God and the Devil. He told me that on that night he and Walt walked home together he…

"But wasn't there a gun on him?" She cut in and asked.

"Yeah and he admitted to the police that he fired it."

"So sad what our kids have to go through," she said.

That comment taking my mind in a new direction.

***

I thought about the money that Mr. Nassy offered me. To be honest I needed it. Adrienne had been on my ass about getting her a ring, but I wanted to buy a car, a particular car. I had been eye-balling a candy red GTO that I saw parked in a front yard on the Westside. The price tag was seventy-five hundred.

I called the phone number written in black marker on the for sale sign attached to the window. I tried my damnedist to talk the owner down a few thousand but he wouldn't budge…I shoulda used my white voice on the phone maybe he woulda been more receptive to my request.

I had money saved for the rainy days that never seemed to stop but for that car, I would spend all I had and just start re-saving again.

My thinking was distorted from being under the pressure of a promise that I would look into a child's death. I wasn't a private detective like the character Easy Rawlin's but now, I could see how he felt in the pages of the Walter Mosely books.

I was deeply connected in the culture of the streets, more than I would ever admit to anyone, especially Adrienne. I pushed the offer of the five stacks to the back of my mind and cemented my decision to help the Nassy's because it was the right thing to do, even if it could cost me my life. As far as the ring and GTO…

***

"I can remember being a little boy, running down the street playing ruff-and-tumble on the tree lawn. We played and ran as hard as we could every day, pretending to be our football heroes, walking, limping and making moves just like them. But they were just men on television, the dudes who played for Southside were real, Garcia Lane, Brian Marrow, Tyrone & Scott Ivy, Ellis Sullivan. I could see them up close, shake their hands and look at their cleats and dirty football pants.

Little Donnie and me used to cut through a backyard of a house on Ellenwood and crawl through a hole in the fence behind the visitor stands to steal a free game. We would stand up against the rail and cheer for Garcia watching him run up and down the field, throwing passes, running back punts, those days were fun, those days formed my life as an athlete… being able to watch, dream and run like Garcia Lane."

We finished dinner and headed off to the seven o'clock movie. I decided to go see Isum again soon, very soon.

Like I ain't got nothing to live
Like as if you had guns to my kids fuck it (going all out)

- Mobb Deep

11

ISUM DUART

ERIE STREET CONNECTED to Delason Avenue, we called that connection the "L" because the sidewalks looked like a large letter L that began right in front of the entrance of Southside High Football Stadium. After the games, the crowd would spill out into the middle of Erie Street and turn it into a party scene until the police would pop off their sirens and yell to move along and go home. Bodies would scatter in all directions like the roaches that got surprised by the sudden shine of a ceiling light.

About a half mile down the L, Delason emptied out into a dark bend under a rusted bridge, so dark that that you would disappear into the triple black shadows. If it's late enough, fiends and prostitutes would run tricks from when the sun went down until the sun came back up. When you made a left on Erie and then a right down Delason, you wanted trouble, unless you happened to live down that way and even then, it could be bad for you. I did my best to stay out from down there especially when I was younger.

***

Thursday after practice, I went back to the Happening House to talk to Isum hoping to get more info from him-way more than I did the before. I again waited for him to come through the big metal door. He sat down.

"What up Coach," he said.

"How you feel Isum?" I asked.

"I'm cool, I guess."

"You better stop guessing and start knowing."

"I'm good Coach, for real."

"Isum I been worried about you, I been praying for you, I come here to see you but to be honest I hate even walking through the front door. I been thinking a lot about our last talk and I decided that I'm going to do whatever I can to help you, but you got to tell me the truth man. Ima be straight with you, the last time I was here you told me basically a bunch of bullshit cause there had to be more going on than what you been telling me."

He slouched back in the chair and folded his hands on the edge of the table. He looked around like he was checking to see if anyone was trying to catch the words of a snitch.

"Coach, it's funny though, because I been thinking about what you said." Isum put his head down as if to gather all of his thoughts.

"About what, I say a lot," I said.

"You know about the vomit thing, dogs go back to their vomit and lick it up. I had a dog once, his name was Bucket.

"Bucket?" I said.

"Yeah Coach, Bucket. I know that name sounds crazy and shit, but I loved that little dog. I don't even know what type of dog he was, he was light brown and had floppy ears. Moms said he was a mutt-I guess that is what he was, a mutt just like me. I found him walking down the street, he was sniffing around some trash, and something made want to take him home with me. He ain't have on no collar or tag so I picked him up and took him to the crib. I called him Bucket cause as soon as we got to the house I put him on the back porch. I went inside to ask if I could keep him, at first she said no, but after she saw him she changed her mind. She started to tell me all the stuff we had to have to keep a dog, you know shots and food and shit, we got caught up talking that's when we walked out to the back porch so I could show her the dog, he was gone. I remember I was upset and shit, I ran outside in the backyard trying to find his little ass. I looked under the car, the bushes, all over the place, then my yelled that she had found him. He was curled up in a bucket asleep. After a while, I just let him have that as his little crib to chill in and that is why I called him Bucket. I put an old towel down in there for some cushion and he would just get in there like a little ball.

Sometimes when he would be out running around in the yard, he would eat grass and I remember one day he was eating that grass and started to choke on it and threw it back up. I thought that little dog was dying or something, but he threw that grass up and then ate it. I ain't never seen no shit like that before. So Coach you think that I don't be listening to you but I do. I read the Bible verses you be giving me… and…I get it, that I can't be like a dog and keep going back to dumb shit in the street… going back means that I never move forward, I need new friends and a new life-if not then I'm eating my own vomit."

Silence seemed to hit the room, all the bustle and noise disappeared for a moment. Isum looked up at me looking for my approval, which I gave him, but with more instruction to follow.

"Good job, you figured it out, I hope, so now, you have to put it into action, take steps to renew your spirit and that can only happen if you remain in the truth no matter what comes your way."

"Like the Apostle Paul right?" Isum asked me.

"Right and exact," I replied with a smile. That was proof that he was reading.

"Coach… there is some stuff I been leaving out that I'm ready to tell you about now, stuff I shoulda told you before but…"

I quickly sat up in my chair and leaned in toward Isum's voice I had been waiting on this conversation that I had always known was tucked away in his head. I was excited but fearful to hear what he was about to say.

"That night that Yosef died, we were headed outta the locker room eating them cookies from the cheerleaders but right before we got to the door Coach B called Yu into his office. I keep walking but I stopped right outside the door cause it was raining all hard, so we waited for him. Yosef was up in there with the whole family. I didn't think much of it at the time, but thinking back I don't know now.

At first it was quiet in there, then you could hear voices. At first I couldn't really hear what they was saying but then Coach B started lightweight yelling at Yosef and Marva. I walked up to the door trying to hear what it was about, but all I could really hear was 'Marva crying and Mrs. B trying to calm Coach down, so I just went back and stood outside the locker room until it was over. I didn't want to get caught with my ear to Coach's door.

Yosef came out, he was upset. The rain had stopped. I gave him a few minutes to calm down and I asked him why was Coach trippin' on him…he put his headphones on, flipped up his hoodie, looked me square in the face and flat out said…"

Isum suddenly stopped and I stole the chance to interrupt.

"Who is we?"

"Yeah Coach, it was me, Walt and Yosef. Walt was outside the locker room waiting for
us."

"Oh-okay," I said.

Isum continued his story.

"He walked out the office and I said, "what's up, what the fuck happened in there, why was Coach all in your shit?

"He said… 'man, whatever I tell ya'll-ya'll can't say shit to nobody. I fucked up, she pregnant man. I don't know what to do, her parents are trippin' making shit worse. Mar' all up in there crying, I couldn't take it so I bounced, man let's go."

"Pregnant," I said back.

"Yeah Coach that what he said, he told us on all that we love not to tell anyone about it, not even you, he begged us not to tell you, it seemed as if he was more worried about what you would say then her being pregnant.

We kept walking getting closer to the back part of the practice field, you know on the side part of the L by Delason Ave. He was jammed up in that shit bad Coach, he was shaking, crying and acting like he was losing his shit, dis niggah started mumbling to himself like-like he was going crazy. I knew he was upset but he was on some different shit. So we walked a little more down the street and he just stops, he turns around and runs back to the locker room. Me and Walt ran after him, but you know that niggha fast as fuck so it wasn't like we could catch him. We pulled up behind and that's when Marva and her parents were coming out of the locker room. Yosef grabbed Marva's hand and pulled her up to the top of the bleachers. Me and Walt ran and stood under the concession stand out of the rain cause fuck-ass Mr. Hall locked the locker room door and wouldn't let us chill in there.

We couldn't hear what they were talking about but you could see that it was on some real serious type shit. Coach B and his wife called for her to come down but she didn't. Coach B and Mrs. B went and got in dey car, me and Walt started to walk home. I was like fuck it-let's be out. I yelled up to Yosef that we would check him later. He said cool and that was it… we left him and Mar' up in the bleachers."

I fell back in the chair in disbelief of what I just heard. It was not the first pregnancy story I ever heard, but this one seemed like a script from a movie, the coach's daughter- the cheerleader- the dead boyfriend- the thug in jail-a rainy night. I had to pull it together so I sat back up, composed myself, and told Isum to empty every bullet of this story to me. We was knee deep in it now, there was no turning back for either one of us.

"We was walking-chiilin' then the rain started back up and whatnot…we was still walking toward the L, looking back at it Coach, we should have stayed there with him that night.

Coach-you know the farther down the L you walk, the darker it gets, we was almost at the end, when five dudes stepped outta know where. They all had on black hoodies so I couldn't see dey faces and shit, but I knew it was some niggahs though Coach. Dey had the draw stings pulled tight so nobody could see dey faces.

I put my hand on Walt's chest so he would stop walking forward. I started backing both of us up and we started tripping over each other's feet. The next thing I know, dis niggah Walt takes off running. I just kept backpedaling as fast as I could-I didn't want to turn around and run and catch a cap. I swung my backpack around to the front and put my hand on the gun in the side pocket, they started running at me and that's when I tripped over the fucken sidewalk.

Next thing I know dey was up on me, these dudes are beating me down, these niggah is kickin, punchin, blam-blam. My hand was still in my backpack. I had the gun in my hand with my finger on the trigger and I pulled it. I shot right through the bag. I fired three times. They all ran. I heard one of them scream, 'I'm hit-I'm hit.'

I got up. I could barely see, caught a kick to the face so my eye was fuck up. I remember stumbling into the fence. I ran back toward the stadium and hid behind the blocking sled on the practice field. My shirt was ripped, face all puffed-up and I was wet as fuck.

I reached in my pocket and pulled out my phone and called Walt…no answer…I called Yosef too…no answer.

Next thing I know coach, here comes the police. Three rollers, sirens blasting and lights flashing. Boom, I hit the wind again. I started running fast a fuck, that's when the cop ran up on my ass. I saw him running my way, I couldn't really see his face, but I knew his voice. He started yelling "drop to the ground Isum… Police… drop to the ground-drop to the fuckin' ground! So that's what I did because I remembered what you told us Coach, you know-cops ain't got a gun for no reason and neither did I, but I dropped that mug quick."

Isum was talking with his hands, as his story got more intense with every word like he was a rapper on a stage.

"Was it Officer Jameson?" I asked him.

Yeah it was his punk-ass," Isum said.

"Jameson," I said.

"It was him and his boy Romano. I hate both dem mutha-fucka's Coach. Don't nobody like them or fuck with them. He act like his son too good to fuck wit us out here. Like we don't wanna get out the hood and go to college.

He act-like Walt is baby Jesus and was gonna throw his life away if he ran with us. I ain't the one his daddy need to be worrying about… Shit, me and Yosef had dreams too, he acted like we were some bums just playing ball with no hope of making it out."

"What do you mean by that last thing you said? I asked. "The part about his dad not having to worry about you, explain?"

Isum starts playing dumb now, saying too much.

"Huh? What you mean Coach?" Isum asked me.

I caught every word that came out of Isum's mouth but now I'm choosing just to sit back and not press the pressing question that now sat idle in my head. I let him keep telling his story the way he wanted to tell it.

"Nothin' Isum, skip that question too, just go ahead I'm listening."

"Cool, see Jameson always played us when he saw us in the street, saying negative foul ass shit about us all the time. That night he caught me, he slammed me to the ground talkin' all low in my ear saying that I killed somebody. I knew I shot one of them but I didn't kill him, he was laying on the ground, and whoever it was he wasn't dead."

"What happened to Walter, did he ever come back to where you were?" I asked him.

"Naw, I guess he slid out when he saw his pops roll up, I didn't see him no more that night… can't blame him though, his daddy is da-poe-poe."

I got up from the table. Words, that a moment ago, made sense to me, were now scrambled letters of confusion in my head. Again, I could feel my temperature going up attached to my heartbeat that was like the sound of beating snare drums in my ears. My vision began to blur causing me to brace the wall. I wobbled as best I could toward the water fountain and reached down into the bottom corner of my pocket for the yellow pill. I looked at it, thought about what my doctor warned me of *"these pills can cause addiction, but you can take them twice a day."*

I stared at the pill in the palm of my hand. The attack getting worse with each second that I stand here and not shove it down my throat because I'm thinking whether or not to take it. *Twice a day, but it can be addictive, what kind of advice was that…*the kind that I was warned about by my uncle, *'they diagnose you, give you pills with a warning, but tell you take it anyway, don't let them drug you up nephew.'*

The pressure, the feeling of fear, death, slowly creeping in, I could see Isum looking at me, as if I was some type of fiend, he was ice-covered in panic at what he saw. He never got up, he just sat there looking at me with concern.

I needed a break in the pace that was building up inside me. I pushed the fountain lever, threw the pill into my mouth and walked back to Isum. I knew that I could last five minutes without falling apart, that the pill would kick and bring me back to life.

"Coach you good?" Isum asked me.

"I'm good, be having to take my pills this doctor got me on, stress and whatnot and this stuff you are telling me now is stressing me out for real. I need nepenthes."

"Whats a nep-n-thes Coach?"

"Nepenthes Isum, it's a drug from Greek Mythology, it's a fictional medicine to get rid of sorrow."

"You got sorrows Coach," he asked.

"Shit-yeah I do Isum, you being locked up in here gives me sorrows and Yosef's death gives me sorrows."

"So you don't want me to tell you the rest?" Isum asked me.

The complaints I had about my doctor's instructions didn't outweigh what that little man-made drug did to my insides, calming me down in an instant moving my non-existent fear of doom far from me now. But, also planting a seed of doubt of the question of *am I getting addicted.*

"We have come too far to turn back now Isum, let's get it all out in the truth, you left off at the part where Walter's father didn't see him there," I reminded him.

"Yeah that's right…yeah then Jameson started kickin' my whole ass Coach, he told me not to move, I was lying on my stomach trying to keep my face out of the muddy water and that's when this dude tried to drown me.

"What!" I said.

"On the real Coach, he put his knee in my back which made my face go in the mud. Then he started punching me real soft in the back of my head- like he was fuckin' wit' me or something, then he pulled me up and cuffed me to the sled. Everything was in slow motion and I could swear that I heard every drop of rain that hit my face.

He got up off me, He told me to relax and sit still and keep quiet."

"Did you recognize the boys that jumped you?" I asked."

"Come on Coach, you know I can't do that part- snitching ain't in me, naw I couldn't see their faces, they had the hoodie strings pulled tight.

I knew I was in it then Coach. I shot somebody."

I was listening and breathing slowly to calm my anxiety and waiting for the pill to kick in. I knew that Jameson was there that night, but he made it seem as if he came in on the back end of it all when according to Isum, Jameson was a major player in what happened. I now began to wonder exactly how major the role Jameson played with Isum and the five boys who showed up that night. I knew that Rick Gaddy was the one Isum shot because he showed up at the emergency room at Saint Elizabeth Hospital that same night. I hadn't run across that name before but I 'm sure this was not the last time I would hear it.

Isum laid his head down on the worn tabletop as if he was tired.

Next to me was that gun, he said.

I shoulda threw it over the fence

'*You ever stare down the face of a gun,*' he asked me like some gangsta-shit. I'm like wow-what type of shit is this… then boom outta nowhere- he chills out, and gone asked me what happened… and then said that no matter what-he would try and get me out of this, but he said he couldn't get me out of the gun charge. Then I said to him- then you can't help me none.

He sat me up straight and I started to tell him what I saw, the whole thing about getting jumped. I never told him about Walt being there either. He said I was lucky he was still close in the area at that time because if some other cops woulda got there before him I might be dead.

Romano put me in the back of the cop car and I just sat there all wet, I was shook Coach no-lie with a busted ass lip and eye."

I looked down at the cement floor shaking my head with my hands on my face. I played back the events of that night trying to piece together a story board I didn't create. I added Isum's story to my own upon my arrival back to the stadium. I was already at home dozing off after watching Friday Night Touchdown on the local news channel. I didn't think nothin' of it, I had become numb to that sound, especially on a Friday night that was until Browbow texted me.

"I know this city is bad, but why did you have to carry a gun and obviously you had it in the locker room," I asked Isum.

Isum's head went up in the air starring at the long florescent lights annoyed seeing that he just told this long story and all I seemed to get out of it was that they had a gun in the locker room.

"You know how it is Coach, growing up in the 'YO' all this crack, man dudes getting shot in the streets because of that shit on the block, all the gangs, Southside-Eastside and Northside."

I had to agree.

"Man we had to protect ourselves. We wasn't all grimy like you might be thinking but we never wanted to get caught slipping either, so when we got that gun, we hid it out of site, we had a way for how we did it. We used to pass it between us whenever we had to make a long walk home after a party, game or whatever. We did it like that so that we always had protection on us if we got in an alone type situation."

He formed a gun with his right hand and pointed at one of the black correction officers who had his back turned to us. "Walt had the gun last, before the game on Thursday, but I went and got it from him because I had to roll to the Knolls PJ's that day and I wasn't going over there cold."

"Damn boy, why Isum, that's dumb to live like that, Walter down with this too?" I asked.

"Hell-nah-but-hell-yeah, his pops would kill him but he still had to live out here too, shit dudes really hate his ass cause of his pops... Coach you sound like this place ain't wild, you know these streets just like I do. And that's the only reason I had that gun on me that night was because we have to walk out here. This ain't the white Boardman suburbs, where kids get rides home or can-can walk home whenever they feel like it night or day."

"Who gave you the gun and don't tell me about no snitchin' bullshit either, I need to know."

Isum paused to think before he answered me, seeing that this crossed over into the forbidden area and may be the cause him getting his ass kicked or killed.

"Coach, you know I trust you, you been like a dad to us out here and I know you not gonna snitch on me- Sonny Reaves let me get it for a lick and I was..."

I had been through a lot of things in my life, most of it still locked up in my mind but these were kids who I loved with all my might and the things I hide inside, mixed with all this is stirring a hurricane up in my mind.

I'm trying figure out how all of this went down. I'm trying to get it all in order, I'm asking myself why would Sonny Reaves give Isum a gun.

"Isum- I gotta go… let's talk next week."

"Ok, Coach… aye Coach."

"Yep"

"Good luck on Friday, I know we gonna win."

"I'll tell the boys you said hello."

"Dang Coach, not hello, that's lame people talk, tell'em I said what- up!" We both laughed as I headed out the door and Isum back to his cell.

The sun was beginning to set and it gave the neighborhood a glowing appearance. I couldn't help but to think about all the words piled up together that Isum told me. I sat down on my porch. Mr. Brinson walked over and sat with me. Mr. Brinson knew me, he knew when he needed to walk across his grass and sit next to his neighbor.

"Remember at Yosef's funeral Antietam, when his grandparents played that song by Donnie Hathaway. He said '*to keep your self-respect and your manly pride, get yourself in gear and keep your stride, and never mind your fears'*… that song wasn't for Yosef son, he was dead, that song was for you… get up and get moving, you know that things ain't right, go talk to Big Browbow and his wife. The police only gon do so much-son, they got a stack of cases that they gotta solve and Yosef's is just another paper under another.

AJ, I'm sure there is more to the story than you already know or have found out. People talk, they can't help but tell things to other people. Negroes talk too much and most of the time it is to our detriment. I can see it on your face son," Mr. Brinson said to me with conviction.

I been hearing about kids getting threatened, even heard there is spose to be fight on Friday," he said.

I began to ask myself questions about what could have happened that night. My heart was heavy again. I went inside directly to my room and sat down on the edge of my bed. The next thing I knew my eyes were closed and my hands raised in evening prayer. I prayed for the strength that I could help Isum somehow, maybe write a letter or testify on his behalf so he can get out of there and try and live as a righteous young man. I prayed to find something, anything that could help Yosef's grandparents get some better closure other than a closed casket and burial plot. I decided on the spot, to dig deeper, to move faster and to reach out further if I had too, even into danger for the truth, with the Lord's help that was my resolution.

The orange-ish purple night sky was down now. Adrienne came over to make me dinner and even brought it up to me in my room. She was cool like that sometimes. She knew that I was hurting inside and that I just wanted to be alone, so she sat the food down, kissed my cheek, turned and left me to my lamentation. I sat for a while looking out the window at the neighborhood. Time passed and I fell asleep with my clothes on.

I sail out on my paper ship
The Sea is made of fire.

-Gil Scott Heron

12

BE EASY

THE NEXT DAY I went to see and old friend of mine, Polidore Croom. Polidore was deaf and his nickname growing up and even now was "Deaf-P." I always wondered if he knew that was his name on the block and if he did-did he approve.

Polidore was a con man. He was into all types of fraudulent schemes, enough to make sure he could consistently feed and clothe himself and keep a roof over his head. I didn't like his lifestyle because I never wanted to see him get locked up but it was what it was.

I was mad at myself for not going to see him a long time ago because even though Polidore could not hear or speak, he always knew what was going down in the street and he was someone I considered a friend from way back. To make it worse I had his number in my phone.

I had a bad habit of not keeping in touch with people I cared about, I was always a day-month-year late with a visit or phone call and the next thing I knew was , so-and-so died, moved away or been locked up.

I considered Polidore one of my good friends, him and his brother "Black Eyed Pee." Black Eye was doing a life bid for murder over a dice game. He lost seventy-five dollars and swore the dude didn't play it back and one thing led to another, he pulled out a gun and shot the dude in the chest four times, all over seventy-five dollars. He was on the run for a month until someone tipped off the cops. The Police found him hiding in his mother's basement folded up in an old unplugged freezer.

We called him "Black Eye Pee" because he had dark rings around his eyes-like a black-eyed pea or maybe more the look of a Raccoon, either way that name stuck to him. His real name was Brandon-Brandon Croom II. I was in college when Brandon went down and I didn't call or even try to write him and still haven't, my bad habits.

Polidore knew Jameson as well as I did, he didn't like him either but knowing Jameson gave Polidore the freedom to skate around trouble from other cops. That was the only favor Jameson did for him.

I was hoping not to have any problems with Poli; I wasn't down for a fight with a deaf dude just because I don't keep in touch but he has always sentimental that way.

What I needed from him would be quick information, nothing that would keep me with him for too long and what I could get from him is more than Jameson ever could. I put that on our history.

The gangsters, old and young never messed with Polidore, probably because who would really mess with a man that couldn't hear or speak, that sacred most around here, to the world people like Poli didn't exist, but to me he did. He was my man from my side of town-one of ours.

He grew up in a corner house on Front Street. Poli was deaf when I met him, which caused me to assume that he was born that way. We met at the Uptown Arcade playing quarter slot video games. His favorite game was Gallica and that was mine too. When I walked into the arcade, he was already deep in space blasting aliens on one-player mode. I stood over his shoulder watching to see how good he was before I dropped my quarter down the slot and joined in with him in the battle for the universe. Each alien ship we shot down he made a grunting sound. I didn't think anything of it because all kids made sound effects while shooting laser beams across the sky. After the game ended with a high score, he reached out to shake my hand. I said my name is "Antietam." He nodded his head and smiled.

I remember waiting for him to tell me his name, he never did. He pulled out a small pocket notebook and wrote his name on it and that he was a deaf-mute, he couldn't hear or speak. Reading that was shocking to me because every kid I knew could hear and talk. I found myself starring at him, like he was from outer space. He looked back at me and smiled again as if he was used to people viewing him like he was animal at a zoo.

From that day on, I became his friend. We learned to communicate with our eyes and hand daps. We came up with a system of fists bumps and stacks, interlocking fingers and snaps like my uncle did in Nam. The system was tight and efficient. We greeted each other with the stack- 'I'm not above you, you're not above me, we're side by side, we're together."

My uncle explained to me that white soldiers and commanding officers deemed any handshake a threat under the misconception that the-dap was a coded language of black insurrection. He said that dap was necessary for their survival. Dap was banned at all levels of the military, and many black soldiers were court-martialed, jailed, and even dishonorably discharged as a punishment for dapping. Me and P used it for our survival too, our survival as friends especially when all that shit that happened under the bridge. Our- dap (dignity and pride) extended into greetings, warnings, meet up times and basic conversation but when we wanted to really rap, we had to write it down.

We ran together every day, sometimes he would come to my house and sometimes I would go to his. He lived with his parents and little brothers, Elibazz, known as "Lil-Bazz," Steven, known as "Out-loud" and his sister Monica."

Polidore's father (Brandon I) was deaf too but seemed as regular as my uncle or any man for that matter, he worked for the garbage department. His mother, Delphonic Croom worked as cook at the Holiday Inn out in the suburbs. Polidore's whole family knew sign language and that was the first time I had ever seen it done in real life. Before that I would only see it on television when a fundraiser was on or a speech by the President.

I wanted to learn it but never asked or tried, what we already had worked, so I never pursued it. Polidore could read lips and that helped with our interactions because I never carried a pen or paper in any of my pockets.

Polidore couldn't play sports like kids with his disabilities can now, times were not as advanced back then, he was looked at as a handicap and that got him into different types of trouble the older he got. His not being able to hear or express his thoughts through words and that irritated him and then he almost every time found himself in a show and prove.

I began to lean on football and he leaned on stealing and fighting. Robert Bell found out about his skills and hired him into the fold and that was the start of his ending. Over time we lost touch until I came back to Southside High to coach football, so I knew I could find him if need be…and need be was now!

I drove to the last place I heard Polidore lived in, the Lincoln Knolls Projects on the Eastside, down the street from Victory High School. I didn't fuck around over here. Southside and Eastside don't mix and if it did, it always ended bad.

The Victory Projects was deep on the Eastside and only the grimiest dudes lived there. This was only my second time ever rolling through these projects. The first time was to see a girl named' Twana Paul and even then, she had to sneak me out the backdoor and I had to drive my uncles Monte Carlo down the street with the headlights off just to get out of there alive.

The old men that loiter outside the buildings said that Polidore was last seen sitting outside the G-building Apartment V98 on top of a white bucket drinking beer. That was the information I had to go on. I drove to the G-building walked up a flight of stairs and knocked on his door.

"Who is it?" A raspy voice behind the door yelled out.

"Coach Jones, I'm looking for Polidore Croom, is he around."

"Yeah hold on," the voice said.

I waited for about five minutes, when Polidore opened the door. His reddened eyes lit up from seeing that it was me his old friend calling on him. He invited me in and that is when the raspy voice at the door walked in from out of the small kitchen. It was Polidore's cousin Stretch. Stretch was a year younger than me and Poli, when we were kids, he was always tagging along no matter where we went. I liked him because he was loyal to Polidore. I wish I had him as a cousin for that same reason. Stretch had a scar over his right eye from some brass knuckles that he couldn't duck; they said he beat the dude with one eye open and blood running over the other that made him a legend in the streets.

Stretch was a Northside dude and seeing him and Polidore hold up in the Victory Projects was strange to my eyes and mind.

"Stretch, what-up," I said.

"What-up Anti-up," he said in his low raspy voice.

"Same shit man, just trying to hunt down Poli that's all."

"We here man, chillin' in the Victory," Stretch said.

"I see."

"Man why-da-fuk you say Coach Jones at the door? Niggah, you Anti-up to me," Stretch said laughing.

"I would have, if knew it was you at the door."

"Man, you big time now-huh?"

"Naw-Stretch, just trying to help these boys not fall into the shit we did back in the day."

"That's peace man for real," he said.

Polidore was sitting at a round table in front of the picture window that looked out onto the street. He waved me over to where he was sitting. He stood up and we dapped, *'I'm not above you, you're not above me, we're side by side, we're together."*

I looked at P's face. His youth still intact behind the hard years and the assumption of the steady flow of weed he smoked but more for his yellowed tired eyes and darkened lips. His hair was grown out nappy, twisted like antennas. He looked healthy but worn like a new pair of sneakers after a couple of hoop games.

He had done a few years up-state for assault. He got into a brawl over a spilled drink. They said P tried to apologize to the man, the man thought P was trying to be funny by not saying any words, so the dude tried to punk him and P ain't no-where near no punk. I'm guessing that after a few minutes someone told old boy that P was deaf, so the man started mocking P. P had experienced enough in his life to know when he was being clowned, so, that added to his anger. P pulled out a blade and sliced old boy across the chest, about 3 inches down from his throat and it was those three inches that got P three years in the penitentiary.

***

He pulled out his phone, and started texting, the notification immediately vibrating in my palm. I was surprised he still had my number and it made me wonder why he never contacted me over the years.

`(P) How r u my friend?`

(ME) I'm good brother, I need some info from u.

(P)What u need, u know if I got it, it's yours to have.

(ME)P, I need to find out why my players got jumped- Isum Duart, Walter Jameson and Yosef Nassy. I need to find out what that shit was all about, I know u can find out for me.

(P)I can tell u now Ant' that fucked me up. Your player gettin killed like that. I heard from my folks that the Gaddy brothers set that whole thing up with some young cats that play for Rayen. The game dun changed Ant, these boys out here don't give a fuck bout nuttin. We ain't even in our thirties yet and the game done changed that quick.

(ME)I know they don't at all. I been suffering P trying to find the truth, u know how I am man. I can't sleep or eat like a regular person cause this shit has been burned in my mind for over a year.

(P)See, Ant-that truth shit ain't gon work out here, these nigghas whole lives are lies. Only thing u gonna find out here, specially if u fucking round with the Gaddy Brothers is a problem for yourself. If I was u I would leave this shit alone man, unless u ready to put your shoulder all the way in this shit, ur boy is dead and buried man, but if u that pressed about it, u know that will do my thang and find out what I can-cool?

(ME)Cool.

He slid a piece of paper from under an old empty pizza box that was on the table and positioned it so he could write on it.

He tore a corner from off the paper and wrote SOUND THE WARNING? on it.

I dapped him. 'I'm not above you, you're not above me, we're side by side, we're together."

I dapped Stretch and I got out of the Victory Projects as fast as I could. This time I had my headlights on, but I drove fast still not stopping for any reason.

I looked at the paper. I figured since he didn't text it to me that meant he didn't want it traced back to him. The stakes just grew higher.

I take this more serious than just a poem.

- Eric B & Rakim

13

MY MELODY

I DROVE WITH the corner piece of paper balled up in my hand. I erased the text message from my phone just in case. I was being paranoid no doubt but I wanted to play it safe. I unfolded the paper-read it, closed it, opened it and read again. SOUND THE WARNING, what did that mean? I pulled over so I could try and solve the riddle that P put me in.

I was beating my brain up with words, faces and names, none of them making no sense. I looked at the paper again and then it came to me. The puzzle piece that fell into my lap, SOUND THE WARNING meant Robert Bell-sound the warning BELL.

Robert Bell was no longer important to me until Poli wrote what he did on this paper. Now he had come back to life. It wasn't like I didn't see him around the way, but I kept our encounters brief I just didn't put myself in his company any longer then I needed to be. I had to be careful, I had a job and a career to protect and being spotted with an experienced big-time dope boy was sure to get me fired or at the least looked at the wrong way.

I hadn't been on St. Louis in years. I think in my psyche I wanted to talk with Robert. I had to admit that he had a profound effect on who I was today.

The street hadn't changed much, bandos as far as the eye could see. The older black folks either died off or moved back down south with family. Robert's house sat alone flanked by four empty lots on one side and one on the other. Fresh siding made his house stand out, the updated double hung windows tightly fitted inside the white trim. It was a far throw from the sun faded wood it wore years ago. A large deck with a step down sauna extended about fifteen feet off the back of the house. In the farthest part of the backyard there were six large dog cages with six big ass pit bulls roaming back and forth.

I parked four houses up the block just in case my car was spotted, I didn't want it to be seen in front of his crib, doing that made me less nervous about being at his house. I walked up the driveway to the side door. I looked down at the water spigot and it made me smile.

At the door stood a big greasy faced black man who I figured to part of a larger security team, this was hood level protection. He wasn't standing like a soldier would because that would be a tip off to an undercover. His posture was casual, slouched out leaning up against the house on the door knob side. We made eye contact. He stood up and readied his feet and hands for my approach.

I counted four heads which could be four potential problem encounters. I changed my walk, I slowed down and shortened my stride to give me more time to see every angle of stance, every facial expression. I kept my hands out of my pockets and made sure that my waist line on my pants was even and not leaning left or right, giving off the impression of the weight of a gun in my pocket. I moved like I had been there before, which was true, but that was years ago as little boy, this was grown man shit.

I walked to within two feet of big greasy. I put my arms out because I knew the routine, arms out for the pat down. The same one the cops use when they pull you over. I thought it was funny that drug security uses the same techniques cops use but we complain about cops all the time, but I guess it's better to be safe than sorry.

"I'm clean man," I said to greasy face.

"You ain't shit until I say you are niggah," he said.

"Man, I need to see Robert."

"Yeah, you and everybody else, he only see people by appointment only, you got an appointment mutha-fucka?"

"Appointment- nah-mutha-fucka, I don't need one of those my friend," I said.

"Who da fuck is you, da mayor, or some shit," he said laughing.

He pulled out a navy-blue walkie-talkie that was clipped right next to the 9mm tucked in his pants.

"Yo-we gotta a dude out wanting to see RB," he said into the microphone.

"Hold up…no visitor's today man…whoever he is tell-em to get the fuck-on."

"You heard dat didn't you mayor, get the fuck on," he said smiling at me.

"Tell him that it's Antietam," I said.

"What…Ant…Ant…who?" greasy asked.

"Man-just tell him it's Antietam Jones…ANT-TEE-TUH-M," I said slowly at the walkie- talkie.

"Did you hear that?" he said back.

"Yeah, I heard it, hold up," the voice on the other end said.

We stood there waiting for a response from the inside. Greasy looked at me and asked.

"What kinda name is that man?"

"A holy one," I said.

I didn't make any sudden moves while standing next to Greasy, he may have been trigger happy or overzealous about his job and make an example outta me. I was already nervous about being here and my paranoia just knew the Feds where on their way to make the bust of the year and I was going to be a part of it. I could the headlines- Southside teacher busted in drug raid.

"He good," the voice said through the speaker.

Greasy face looked at me in my eyes and opened the heavy steel door. I walked up the short set of stairs and was directed through the kitchen into the living area. Robert was sitting a black leather recliner with his feet up watching television on what looked like a seventy-five-inch flat screen. He turned toward me and smiled, the type of smile that a father smiled upon his long-lost son. He jumped up from his seat and hugged me with strength as to make sure I felt the love he had for me.

I sat down across from him. My eyes swirled around the room taking in all the fancy shit that drug money could purchase, things my teacher's salary could never afford.

"Can you still run?" he asked me.

"Hah, not like I used too," I said.

"Me neither," he said back laughing.

"Rob…I need your help my friend. I know we ain't kicked it in years but I need a solid."

"Years don't mean shit to me Ant, me and you will always be close, I know you got a different life than I do, and I respect what you do brother…and that's real-talk."

I took a deep breath from his words as they relaxed my brain and let me get straight to the point.

"Rob, I'm trying to find out some information about Yosef, you know info that aint been found for over a year. I ain't sure why I'm still digging around about it but I am. So…I'm coming to you cause I know you stay locked in around here."

"Yeah Ant that was some sad shit about Yosef, he could play the game, damn near was better that you…my only question to you is this…why you wait so long to come holla at ya boy?"

"Man…life that's all…life been getting in the way," I said.

"Understood."

"I need to find out who I can talk to about what really went down that night Yosef was found dead."

"Jameson's punk ass ain't do shit all these months?" Robert asked.

"He tried when this first happened, but the case was closed a while back and I sorta let it go myself, I be frontin' for people, like the shit ain't eating me up inside, especially when I lay down at night. Yosef be haunting me like a ghost."

"I bet man…that had to be some hard type shit to deal wit."

"The hardest ever up to this point in my life- no doubt."

"Even harder when Unc and Lil Donnie died?" He asked.

"Different, but harder."

Robert declined and scooted to the edge of the recliner. His forearms resting across his legs.

"Ant-you know I got love for you. Outta any mutha-fucka's in this trap ass city that I would help, it's you. I'm glad you came to me. I had to cut this niggah lose years ago. He was starting to think he was bigger than me, niggah lucky I didn't have him offed."

"Who?"

"You know the niggah too, Haso Thomas. He fucks around with little petty ass dudes, got them selling weed and shit for him, he dabbles lightweight in caine too. I know for a fact he got a few football players working the school hallways. I hate to say it, but you asked me for help. If I was you I would go to that niggah and ask him to his face. No worries Ant, he ain't gone do shit, he soft as fuck. Go see him and make him cough up dem answers you looking for."

"Haso Thomas?" I said.

"Yes sir…"

"Will I need a gun?" I asked.

"Man-he ain't cut like that Ant."

I thanked Robert and left out the same way I came in. I head nodded grease face and walked back to my truck. I sat in silence thinking of the plot that just got weaker than before.

***

Haso Thomas move to the top of list. Bell said that I knew him but as hard as I tried to pull his face up in my mind, I couldn't. I hadn't gotten as much as I hoped with Polidore other than the lead to Robert and I was getting frustrated so much so that I was considering going back on my promise I made to the Nassy's.

I was too far removed from visiting grown ass men in the projects and looking at day-old pizza boxes that stacked up on lopsided tables. I had lost that part of my make-up when I went away to school. That section of my character had lost himself in psychology books and ice coffees at the student center on warm spring days. An educated man should not have to drive his car in fear down a one-way street hoping not to get car-jacked by the time he reaches the corner. What was I doing…I asked myself.

There would be no more project visits for me, no more dank ass kitchens to sit in. I wasn't a private detective and no one was paying me to do a job I wasn't trained to do. If I could not find an end to all this then the Nassy's, Coach Browbow, and the whole community, we will all have to live with doubt and Yosef may never rest in peace.

I didn't know no-damn Haso Thomas. I had heard his name on the backend of hood talk, but didn't have any encounters with him until now, and that is still up in the air.

I backtracked a step and sent Polidore a text.

(ME) What-up P I need to get word put out to some dude named Haso Thomas. Bell told me to reach out to him about the stuff we talked about-can u send a kite for me?

(P) I can do that for you, Ant, you know this dude?

(ME) Rob said I do, but I don't think I do.

(P) Be careful my-dude, where u want to link up at?

(ME) Have him come to my crib, tell him I wanna make a weed purchase, I will shoot u my address in a few.

(P) Coo...

I knew Poli would make this happen for me. I knew that this was probably not the right way to handle this situation putting my reputation on the line but at this point, I was desperate and reaching for any angle from all ends.

I sent Polidore my address, Haso agreed to come to my house which in hindsight was just another bad idea, but I wanted him to feel comfortable being in my space and not looking over his shoulder the entire time and it was better than being on some dark ass side street or dim lit parking lot, looking like we making a major drug transaction. If was to shoot me or something I figure it would be better to be shot in my driveway rather in the alley.

Haso pulled in my driveway right before dark. He had a nice car as about as nice as the one Robert Bell drove back in the day. I walked out and met him. The closer I got I could see that Haso was a large man. He looked about 280 pounds but was only 5'7 and being at the short made him look even rounder-Jaba the hut round.

The hood-wits that I still had moved my eyes immediately to the backseat of his car. I wanted to make sure he was alone. I didn't need any niggahs jumping out and trying to bang on my head. He had a dime bag sitting on the passenger side seat next to a chrome 9mm pistol. The strong smell of the purple smoothed my nose.

"Coach Antietam Anthony Jones?" he said with his face covered by the brim of his baseball cap.

"Yeah, you Haso?"

"No, doubt the one and only. I'm feared by bandits, hated by chicks, loved by kids and I never did a bid. The football coaches buy weed too huh," he asked.

"Nah-not really, I just really need to talk you about a few things."

"Look here Coach. Haso don't have time to waste, I don't know what's up, but ya-man's said you wanted a bag. I got da bag-it's twenty."

"I know that what this is supposed to be, but I need to get some info from you."

"Info, I ain't got no info for a niggah like you."

"Haso, listen here my-man…I'm trying not to come out of my hook-up. I left that life a long time ago. I don't want no problems man, I'm just a plain old football coach and teacher, that's all man, I don't want no weed but I heard that you are the one who serves the kids at the school or should I say you the one who got kids serving for you. True or not, I need to ask you a question and then you can get the fuck out my yard."

I hated when I had to go back in time and act out what I hated about myself, but Haso didn't appear to understand anything else.

"Miss-me with all that tough talk niggah, ask yo question."

He leaned his seat back more than it already was and looked up at me with a sideways eye.

"Haso, do you know Isum Duart?"

"Yeah, that's my little homie, why?"

"You know he locked up right?"

"Yeah I know, he popped a niggah."

"Yeah he did, did you see him, the night Yosef Nassy got killed? I asked him.

"That was the football player-wasn't it? Spose to had been real good too I heard. Naw man-nowhere near that scene."

"Haso, I need you to think back, this is important to me, important to that dead boys family, you know what I mean. I don't smoke, I don't want to buy nothing off you, I had Deaf-P hit you up cause people said you might be able to put some pieces together for me."

"I hear you-I hear you. I probably was laid up with one of my ladies that night, you know."

He leaned forward as far his belly would let him, putting the dime bag of weed into the glovebox along with the pistol. I guess feeling at ease now.

"You don't remember me do you Ant'?" He asked.

I stepped back to better my focus of his bubble shaped face. He looked familiar but I know a few fat boys and like I said before I ain't in the habit of keeping up with people, and definitely not a dude like Haso Thomas."

I stood there trying to recall his face.

He took off the cap he was wearing and looked at me square.

"Dam Ant' it's me Fat Toney," he said.

"Fat Toney, hell-naw, it is you ain't it?"

"No-doubt," he said. "Niggahs don't call me Fat Toney no-mo, I'm 'Mega' now."

"Mega-okay, I got you, but if it's cool, Ima just call you Haso."

"That's the name moms gave me," he laughed.

Now that he revealed who he was, I went in for the kill because regardless if he called himself Mega or whatever, he will always be Robert Bells fuck-boy Fat Toney to me.

"Haso, I apologize for not recognizing you but it's been a long time since we seen each other. We can catch up another day, but right now I need you to put me on with what I asked you."

"I shoulda told who I was off-rip, but aihgt-Ant, see, your boy Isum owed me some money. He was my weed connect in the school-house. He started coming up short-n-shit with my ends and like any self-respecting weed man and that was a problem.

See, them boys he got into that beef with that night, dey my-lil' dudes. Isum got South on lock and Craig Cotton got the other spot."

"The other spot Ima guess is Rayen High," I asked.

"Ima let you figure that out bruh…See, Ant Ima keep it real with you. I don't give a fuck 'bout no football and all that shit, that's your area, my area is dese streets. I don't care what grade a niggah in, none of that, niggah wanna sell my product then he responsible for everything that come with it. I sell weed cause that shit aint gon kill nobody. Crack, herion I don't fuck with all like that, that shit killin mutha-fuckas man and I ain't trying to live with that shit on my conscience or catch no charge casue some cluck O-D'd on me.

Isum fucked up my bread so I told Craig to…you know…send him a message, just so happened that it went down on the same night yo-mans Yosef got killed or whatever the fuck people say happened to him."

There are times when you want information, an answer to a hard question, but when you get it, a part of your mind regrets even asking for it. This was one of those situations. I didn't want to hear that my football players or any kid for that matter is out here selling weed. But right here in my driveway was a man telling me that he has football players selling for him inside the school. My right mind said to call the cops, but I gave my word that this meeting was not about the law, so to that word I will keep.

"Haso, I appreciate you telling me the real. It helped me out a lot."

"You sure you don't want this bag man, you looking stressed out, this shit is medicine too," he said.

"I'm good, stay safe out here Haso."

"You too Ant, oh yeah, one more thang, this might sound like some bitch type shit but I think your boy Yosefs girl was tippin' out on him. I overheard Craig hollerin bout knocking off the coach's daughter…damn Ant, she get down like that?"

"What the fuck you talkin about Haso," I asked him.

"Fuck-you-mean, you heard what I said, that niggah said he was fucking your boy's girl."

"Man listen, I said I appreciate the info, but all this other shit you talking about, ain't my business anyway," I said in a semi-loud voice.

"Just saying bro, just sayin."

I pressed pause.

I looked over the roof of his car at the bando next door. The moon was shining giving the bando a holy azure glow that brought a little life to its emptiness.

"Im out Ant," Haso yanking me out of my blue fantasy.

"Cool, I appreciate your help man."

"Whatever," he said dissing my thanks I forwarded him.

I cleared my feet back far enough so he could pull out of my driveway.

He backed up slowly, careful, creeping inch by inch as not to cause the front of his car to dip and bang the peak of the incline where the bottom drive and sidewalk meet. He ripped up the street barely slowing down at the stop sign that was decorated with bullet dents.

Craig Cotton and Marva washed around in my head. I didn't want to believe what Haso told me about her. I had to stop and remember that they are teenagers and teenagers go from relationship to relationship, and maybe Marva was no different. Maybe my real worry wasn't her but what that rumor would do to her father. That was selfish of me to think but it did cross my mind.

I stood outside for a few minutes digesting what I predicted would be the next episode of this circus, I called my life. My peripheral vision caught curtains swaying from noisy neighbors looking out their windows. Even though my neighbors watched me grow up, they all know I graduated from college and teach and coach, they still peek at me behind the edges of window panes and from chairs in dark bedrooms. I stood a few minutes more, the street was quiet and the bloodthirsty mosquitoes started to attack.

This-talent that I got will resound the spot.

- Old Dirty Bastard

14

HUTCH

I HAD DEAF P and Haso on my mind, one I loved and the other I thought nothing of, but both playing minor roles in a story that was still folded up like an envelope.

***

I got up earlier than usual because I wanted a little time to talk to Jameson about Isum. He was sitting at his desk to the right of the front doors. His head was down and he was writing, the squeak of me opening the door alarmed him.

"Damn Ant, you up early, you scared me; this ain't the time you usually get here."

"Yeah I know, I rolled up here early because I need to rap with you for a few."

"Ah-shit, okay, I'm listening," Jameson said as he started setting up orange cones along the steps.

"I went up to the Juvie last night and spoke with Isum and he laid some heavy shit on me about that night all that shit went down."

"Damn man, why can't you just let it go brother, he is dead man, let the dead rest. You might believe this, but I feel sorry for you Ant, a whole year has passed and you still searching for answers-where there ain't none. I know I come like I don't give a fuck about certain shit but I do.

People been speculating about what went down with Yosef, rumors saying suicide-can't see that, he owed some drug dealers money-can't see that either, but I can see, him being pushed, or maybe it was just an accident which is what I believe in my heart. Either way Ant' it's a cold case now, sorry to say that to you but it is what it is.

I know it's hard to accept because it's hard for me to accept, but you listening to Isum Duart, dumb ass Isum Duart, the same dude who stay in and out of trouble? He trying to save his ass, he looking at two years maybe three, he almost killed that kid man, I even tried to help him out of that shit. I tried to hit the prosecutor on some side shit with self-defense plea for him but they jammed him up with felonious assault and for him that may as well be a death sentence.

I mean what the fuck he gonna do when he get out. A black man with a felony, no real education, I mean what chances does he really have out here? He gonna end up being another niggah I gotta chase up and down the block until either I retire or he gets tired of running. You don't know what that shit feels like-having to arrest an old classmate or teammate, or what's worse, arresting dey parents?"

"Yeah, he told me that you said you would try and help him the night all this happened, but he also…" Jameson cutting me off.

"Because I did, I meant what I said, listen bro' I know me and you ain't never really been cool all like that, and I know I been on you about my son getting the ball but that's because I want the best for him. But this Yosef shit… man… you gotta let it go, whatever Isum told you may or may not be accurate-but I'm telling you, as far as Yosef goes, he was found face down, face down in that puddle- face down not moving, with a busted head. They think he hit his head on a beam as he fell and that is what killed him. Now, true or not-don't matter, all that matters is that he is resting in peace and if you start asking questions his peace is being disturbed.

I know this shit is close to you but this coulda happened to anyone. That stadium is old as fuck and all that shit is falling apart, shit was old when we played there. The detectives that were assigned to his case said that the screws were loose on the railings. The city don't give a damn about that stadium, the school district obviously don't give fuck, man when was the last time it's been inspected for any safety violations before someone had to die?

Man, look around this place, we live in a city full of bandos man. Now, if he jumped then that's a whole-nother conversation, a conversation that people in this town don't want to talk about or even think about. We can't push that theory on those two old people that raised Yosef. Let that boy be dead from what is wrote on his death certificate… *accidental fall.*

When I got the call and dispatch said that we had a dead body at the school, my heart dropped to my feet, I had just left there fuckin' around with Isum's dumb ass, cause he wanna shoot guns and shit, and then, I pull up and see Yosef lying there dead.

People don't give a fuck about the cop's man and all the shit we gotta go through every day round here. Think about what I went through that night Ant'? First, we have a shooting after the game, then I have to arrest a kid I have known since he was a little boy and then hours later there I was back up at the field where I played at trying to save Yosef's life.

All that shit within 24 hours! What I'm saying is this-if the fall didn't kill him, then the water that his face laid in did.

I spoke with several people about this case, my captain, the coroner, public defender, all off da-record, and all of them tried to make sense of it but it is what it is, and what I just told-I ain't supposed to be tellin', so right there should let you know that I'm deep in this just like you. I hate seeing another dead kid out here, Yosef and Walt Jr. the same age, shit, that coulda been my son out there laid face down in the rain alone."

***

I left Jameson in the hallway, and walked up to my room and found a card on my desk that read Good luck tonight Coach and God Bless. From Mrs. Browbow. The gesture made me feel better and I knew that Mrs. B understood what this day meant, not only to me but to the entire community.

The first bell rang and you could hear the doors opening to welcome the students into class. Slowly the hallways filled with kids most wearing the school colors. The cheerleaders were dressed in their uniforms and the football players in their game jerseys. The school was buzzing with spirit in anticipation of tonight's big game. At schools like this you have to cherish rival games because that is the only time school spirit is in full effect. Other than that, no one hardly even comes to the games.

I was leaning on the wall with my arms folded waiting for all of my students to come in. I could see the dawning of number sixteen weaving in and out of the crowded hallway. It was our quarterback Hutch Campbell.

Hutch was six foot one and weighed close to one hundred and eighty pounds. He was handsome like Yosef. His skin was a deep brown that played well with the waves in his hair that he brushed constantly. His face was strong and projected confidence of an adult man.

Hutch was a pure athlete having all the attributes that any coach would want for a quarterback and captain. He was fast and quick. He was agile and powerful. He could catch as well as he could throw. He had great field vision and awareness and was accurate with every route. He was the quarterback I thought I was.

His accolades came deservingly. He was an All-American and had colleges kicking down Coach Browbow's door to get him on their campus.

He understood the pressures of trying to be perfect. He practiced his perfection by going to class and not getting into trouble, that's the nature of the position I used to tell him, it was the stereotype that white high school Qb's mastered all too well, it was our kids who couldn't grasp what the title of quarterback demanded, but Hutch Campbell did. The Qb's at those elite white schools were taught how to blend leadership and academics and if they were lucky enough to be handsome, than that made it all the better. I made sure that Hutch not only understood that but acted it out. It wasn't that I was trying to make him like those white players but being a black quarterback was never really popular or accepted. I played that role when it was on me to lead my team, and now, it was Hutch's turn.

He came by to see me because I was his positon coach and the offensive coordinator and I made sure that he and his two backups Kevin Harris and Greg Brown came to see me every Friday morning during the season just to make sure there all three were ready with the game plan.

***

Hutch lived up-the-hill, just him and his mother, his parents divorced a few years ago, but his father was still a heavy presence in his life which

I was happy about and that meant that he was one less boy I had to worry about not having a father figure in his life.

He wanted to be a coach like me, he looked up to me, I could tell. He wore number sixteen because I wore that number years ago when his father would take him to the games to watch me in action. Things came full circle with Hutch. I was Hutch's Garcia Lane of times past. He hung on every word that I spoke about football, so I was always careful in which way I led him. I took my relationship with Hutch to heart; he and I spent many hours talking especially over the past year after what happened to Yosef and Isum. Hutch gave me hope and made my sorrows over Yosef's death easier to deal with; I needed Hutch to fill a void.

"Coach, wish Yosef was here tonight, with him out there we would dawg them fo-sho."

"Yes sir, now that I believe,"

"But my boy Walt is holding it down," Hutch said.

"Walt is doing a great job, he is in a tough spot taking over for Yosef and having to deal with some of the pressure his father puts on him."

"Yeah Coach, his pops be going off, bad mouthing the coaches, always got something negative to say. How do you deal with that type of stuff?"

"I don't, when you become coach, like I told you before, you will always have critics, you will always have boos from the stands. You will always have men who come to games, whether they have a kid on the team or not, they might be alums or just high school football fans, but their main objective to talk shit. They pay to get in just to sit in the stands who try and pick apart every call you make, every player you put in the game, or don't put in, but not one of them never been on a sideline doing anything other than maybe as a player back in the day and that makes them experts in the game of football."

"Well, Ima still be a coach after college, hopefully I can work for you. You should have your own team by then, or maybe Coach B will retire, he getting old."

"Yeah he is getting up there in age and no doubt, like I told you before if I'm coaching, you got a job." Hutch shifting gears. "Coach you know what the word on the street is, that a bang-out is going down after the game, dudes been talkin' all types of trash, sending messages through girls and what-not, talkin about breaking my leg… but I'm good Coach… I ain't trippin, just thought you should know."

Hutch smiled and asked for a pass to first period.

Now I'm daydreaming about having my own team. I learned a lot of great coaching under Coach Browbow and hoped one day to be able to put it to the test. I would hire a kid like Hutch Campbell, he could be trusted and depended on the same way Browbow trusted and depended on me.

I'm worried about this game and this sudden addition of drama added to it. Somewhere inside all of this chaos lied the truth, players getting threatened, police leaving parents in confusion, all madness… and to make it worse, ain't no answers in sight.

I'm feelin' this, I'm young and ruthless
Status unmatched, undisputed, some assuming
My destiny to rep these streets
I'm built for this, the will is too strong

- Cormega

15
GAME TIME

MARVA WAS WAITING at the locker room door with the rest of the cheerleaders standing behind her. Their coach, Nicole Arnold holding an arm full of decorations. It was my weekly job to let them in the locker room after it was clear of any players.

"It stinks in here Coach Jones, for real," Nicole said while covering her nose.

"Hey ladies," I greeted them.

"Haaaay Coach Jones," the girls giggled.

"It's a locker room Coach, it's supposed to stink," I said.

"I know but dang," she said laughing.

Nicole Arnold was my first childhood crush. We had known each other since were little kids. I first met her at church. She was sitting with her mother and father and I was with my uncle during one of the few times we went to church. Thinking back on it, it was Veterans Day. Nicole's father had been in the Navy so we had that in common. I didn't have any female friends back then, but she grew on me as we got older and she turned into the sister I never had.

She was always pretty and the neighborhood boys tried their best game on her but it never worked. She was a tom-boy and that gave her an edge on the average brotha trying to get at her. Her eyes were golden like honey on a spoon and if the light hit them at the right angle, they would glow like diamonds dipped in melted butter in the sunlight.

Coming up, we played all the school sports that a boy and girl could play. I was on the football and basketball team and she was on the cheerleading and softball team. We both made All-Ohio in high school. We both loved our school. We both went to college to become teachers, she studied elementary education. We both made a promise to come back here and work in this school district. When I got on as an assistant football coach, she got on as the head cheerleading coach.

She never lets me forget that she became a head coach before I did. She was good for the girls of the school-they looked up to her.

***

Each cheerleader had an assigned locker for the season. They filled each one with candy and cookies wrapped in individual plastic bags. Red, blue and white balloons taped above each locker door.

All season long Yosef's locker remained empty until that day. Marva decided to resurrect her routine she had been doing for two and a half seasons. She stood up on her toes doing her best to see up above to the top shelf of the rusted red locker, focusing in on the magnetic name plate that had her boyfriend's name on it…Yousef Nassy #27. She placed five treat-filled bags neatly in order, aligning one after the other. She straightened out his jersey on the hanger and re-folded his game pants and centered them on his stool. She made sure there was no candy paper or grass anywhere in or near his locker.

To all else that locker was off limits. It was a shrine to Yosef, a place of homage to him, never again for a players use, for as long as Big Browbow, or any coach, who knew Yosef, and what he meant to Southside High School, that was hallowed ground.

One day a freshman sat on Yosef's stool to tie his cleats and he almost got his clothes ripped off his body from all the yanking and snatching he received.

Nicole stood and supervised her girls as they worked to get each locker done. I watched Marva closely, our eyes caught and I nodded approving that what she was doing was a good thing. All season she avoided that locker, walked around it and barely looked at it, finding any alternate route she could find, to act as if it was not there at all. But today she stood tall and proud to bless that space as she once had.

After she was done, she reached down into her purse walked over to her coach and asked her to pin Yosef's football button on her. I felt the emotion of the moment and it made me miss him even more.

***

In the cafeteria at the pre-game meal, Big Browbow addressed the team and the importance of tonight's game. He reminded them about the rivalry and the bragging rights we have had over the past three seasons for beating the Rayen High Tigers. He talked about the importance of playing with honor for their fallen teammate.

Coach Johnson and Goodwin simultaneously yelled "don't forget about Isum." Browbow drove home the points of representing the community in the right way by not getting caught up in the trash talk of a heated rivalry.

We all knew the backdrop. We all knew that for centuries that these two schools hated each other and that hatred once involved only fist, knives and bats, but now it was a few fist and lots of guns. The air was still with silence, the intensity grew with each second that there was no sound.

Hutch Campbell stood up and broke the calm.

"Fellas, we gotta win tonight, and like the coaches said, we gotta remember 'Yosef and Isum, they still part of the team and we gotta represent for them. Rayen ain't better than us, but we gotta play hard each play… we 'gotta play hard for the coaches, they believe in us and we believe in each other. I love yall dudes" loud claps erupted.

Next, the other captain T-lee Chism stepped forward and started the team chant, raising his hands high in the air and bouncing up and down until every player was on their feet in unified frenzy. "Warriors-warriors-warriors." They were now ready to play.

***

The temperature at game time was sixty-four degrees. The autumn weather growing inches closer to winter with each gust that came across my face. The atmosphere was electric. There was a nervous intensity that we all could feel with each body that bought a ticket.

The bands played as loud and as hard as they could, one tying to out-do the other. The dance teams swayed and popped in rhythm to the sounds that kept them in step. The cheerleaders screamed cheers to all who could hear.

Both teams entered through opposite tunnels. We had on our red home jerseys and royal blue pants with the wide red stripe down the leg and Rayen in white jerseys and burnt orange pants.

The announcer called out the starting lineups, which gave the stadium a playoff atmosphere. This was the show time. Big Browbow swayed back and forth in the tunnel holding the team back until Rayen emerged from the dark tunnel on the visitor's side. The crowd was getting bigger and bigger and it was already body to body in the bleachers. The fence was jammed packed with spectators jockeying for a good position to see the action of the game.

"Here we go boys," he yelled loudly as he released them into midst of the bands tunnel.

"Kick-return team in the box!" shouted Coach Greene over the booming noise of the crowd.

The announcer said "here we go folks-the Southside High Warriors versus the Rayen High Tigers for it all." The crowds exploded in cheer.

This game, in this small valley, a valley that hides in the shadow of a closed down rusted steel mill, now had life to it, even if for only the length of a high school football game.

These two identical schools on the opposite sides of town both poor, but prideful, tied in a fierce rival game that had in the setting a yearlong noiseless mourning for one of their own, a mourning that no one spoke of and that still shook everyone on all sides. The City Series league was one of the best in North East Ohio. Every team had top players and could have easily been in the same position as the Southside High Warriors and the Tobias Rayen Tigers but this year belonged to them. Next year would have to wait for North Heights High, Victory High and John Wilson High School to try a play for it all.

***

Rayen placed the ball on the tee. The referee blew the game into play. Thunderous roars from the fans swarmed into my ears and I could feel that feeling that I felt years ago when I was under center on Friday night under these same lights.

Rayen's kickoff team aligned eleven across beating their pads in sequence before the ball was kicked. The kicker got his foot under the ball and it sailed high as the white stripes chased each other toppling through the air.

We returned it to the twenty-three yard line. I reached out blindly and grabbed Hutch by the collar and as I always did. My eyes were looking down at my play call sheet trying to find the best play to call to open up the game with.

"Twins-left-twins-left-28 cougar right- twins-left-twins-left-28-cougar-right. Make sure everyone is set, protect the ball."

"Got it Coach," Hutch said back with confidence.

Hutch jogged to the huddle. I could tell they were ready to go due to the shaking and shuffling of their feet as he bent over to relay the play I just gave him. His head was shifting from right to left, his finger was pointing in the faces of his teammates.

Hutch waived his arms like a bird to silence the crowd. A murmured hush blanketed the stadium. He executed his stance; he readied his hands and feet to receive the snap. He was setting the defense with his posture. His eyes were forward on the two linebackers that mimicked his position, then, he stood erect to scan the defense one more time before putting the game into motion. He readied again. I gave him the freedom to check out of the play that I called but only if his eyes told him the truth. The defense aligned exactly how we practiced all week.

"Set-Set…Ready…Set go," Hutch barked out.

The snapped was waist high; Hutch worked his feet at the proper angle, Walter patiently jabbed left and Hutch handed the ball off as he rode Walter into the hole. Walter put himself in the back pocket of the pulling tackle that led him up the guts of the defense. We gained four yards.

In games like this one, every yard counts, that is said about every football game that is played, but this game had higher stakes. Stakes like racing for Robert Bell.

The game was tight. We found ourselves in a tug-of-war matchup. Every quarter was a fierce battle of wills, not giving an inch of grass without a violent exchange of hits. The fourth quarter was upon us. The game had become what many had hoped it would- a last minute thriller. The score was close, close enough to cause the coolest person to come out of that bag. We had put together a long drive and were in position to score.

Coach Browbow called our last time-out.

"Dial up a good one Coach we-in that moment," he said.

The moment he was talking about, was the moment of win or lose. That time where fast intelligent decisions had to happen. I had studied my craft. In the off seasons, I attended clinics with other coaches, learning, watching and listening, all for games like this one. It was funny or maybe strange, in times like this, I never needed that yellow pill, my heartbeat at its regular pace.

***

From the bottom bleachers of the stadium a man in Southside colors antagonistically leaned over the railing and shouted obscenities at me until his soda he was holding began to spill out on his hand.

"Hey Jones, your play calling stinks. I remember watching you play and you choked then, like you gonna choke now."

I wasn't sure wait the fuck he was talking about I never choked, I was a play maker and always made the big play for us. I let him get under my shield for a second; I quickly glanced over my shoulder to see him surrounded by a sea of red and blue. He was in hostile territory even though he was on our side of the stands. He thought that his sentiments about me were universal, when in actuality he was just one of a few haters that probably lived in that world of a has-been jealous spectator. I had to ignore him; it's time to get myself refocused.

"Quiet, calm down, everybody take a deep breath, deeper than you ever took before. Now listen to me, this is it. This is what we worked all year for, for the offense to win the big game for this team. Do your job. If you haven't done your job all night or all season, then dammit do it now…understood?"

Confidence was in their eyes. They were smiling at me and that was a good sign that no fear was in their hearts. We could get this done and I gave them the plan on how we would pull this off.

Hutch's heels sat five yard behind the center Mario Ford. He again waved for the crowd to silence. I was excited for Hutch to be in this time and space. He earned the right to be in the light of the cities attention. Yosef would be proud of him. Yosef would play hard for a leader like Hutch. Yosef would want Hutch to have the ball in his hands and win it or lose it with the best player on the team. Isum would be cheering from the sideline after playing a great defensive game. Even those jealous haters would never show or admit it, but deep down inside past all that evil in their stomachs, they wanted Hutch to sparkle too.

Hutch looked over the orange and black defense that had a desperate apprehensive pose. Todd Finley and Dupee Wilkins stared Hutch down ten feet away from their linebacker spots.

I know he relished the chance God was giving him. He prepared his hands for the snap, this play that he was about to run, we had run all week at practice, so he was ready-we were ready. Hutch had scored both our touchdowns and with those fourteen points we still trailed by four, and one more score by Rayen could put the game out of reach.

He looked at the game clock, a minute-ten-seconds it read. It was third down and two from the plus 17 yard-line. He woofed out the cadence, he got a good snap and began the execution of the play. He took two short pass drop, eyes downfield, but really on the linebackers, waiting for them to turn their backs to him. He pulled up and attacked the middle of their defense. He ran past the backers and had a clear lane to the end zone. He went in untouched and clean, because he was Hutch Campbell. QB draw executed to perfection.

We went up 20 to 18 to a deafening crowd that was at the fences edge ready to storm the field in celebration of the City Series Championship. Our kicker, who everybody called E, missed the extra point which forced us into the hot oven of pressure to play great defense to seal the victory.

The clock was now down to fifty-eight seconds. "Kick-off team in the box." Greene rallied the players around him. "Stay in your lanes, ya'll hear me? Stay in your lanes, break down and make the damn tackle, this shit is big right now fellas."

E aligned the ball on the tee, got a good start and kicked the ball to the fifteen-yard line. Rayen returned it to the twenty-eight, 41 seconds on the clock. The crowd standing on their tiptoes locked in with all the enthusiasm of what was unfolding in front of them..

Rayen runs two plays for a first down, ball on their forty-five yard-line. The clock is down to 30 seconds. Toss sweep to the outside for a twenty-three- yard gain putting Rayen on our thirty-six yard line, 23 seconds to go. Rayen runs for no gain, 14 seconds, second and ten yards to go. Rayen's quarterback Tony Thompson throws an incomplete pass, they call time out. 9 seconds left, facing a third and ten attempt to score. Eddie Blockson sprints off the line on a ten yard out route, makes the catch for a first down. Rayen calls their last time-out with 5 seconds left in the game.

I looked around 360 degrees trying to capture everything in snapshot. I became witness to the black and brown faces, young and old that were scattered in both crowds. I picked out the white people that were brave enough to mingle in like speckled dots of white paint. The leaves that subsided from the surrounding trees danced from sideline to sideline from the breeze that kicked them along. The referees whistle was the only thing that snapped me out of my contemplation.

Rayen sends their field goal kicker onto the field. Red and blue versus orange and black are at a fever pitch of screeching, stomping and shouting. Last play… the snap is good…the kick is up…but falls short. We win!

All the air deflated from my lungs. I looked over at Coach Browbow and we shared a smile, then a hug. My coaching career flashed before my eyes and I thought about all the kids who came through the program, some good, some bad but all Warriors. I thought about my uncle and wished he were here to see me doing my thing. I turned to find Adrienne in the crowd. Our eyes met and I became filled with pride. I ran onto the field and got in line right behind my quarterback

In the midst of the madness of storming fan bodies, each team came together at mid-field to shake hands. Hutch Campbell led our line of forty-five. Craig Cotton, Rayens captain, was the first in line.

As Hutch approached him Cotton said, "good game niggah, to bad your boy Yosef missed it." For a moment, it stunned him. He paused in his steps and I walked up his back. I leaned forward to his ear and told him to keep walking. I could tell that his mind jumped into fight mode, but he knew a fight would cause a riot on this field, so he did as I asked and kept walking down the line saying "good game-good game" but now in an inaudible mumble."

We started down to the home end zone with the rest of the team in tow. My throat was stuck with jumbled up words not knowing how to get them out into Hutch's ear. We walked for about fifteen steps giving me time to loose what was stuck.

"I'm proud of you for how you played today and how you just handled that situation," I said.

"Coach, I was straight about to flip-out right there on the field. That dude Cotton always talking shit…if I didn't have a scholarship on the line I woulda punched his ass on the spot."

"Shit Hutch, I wanted to punch his ass too, but I would straight be in a meeting on Monday trying to explain why I hit a kid, then I would be looking for another job," I said laughing.

"Hah-yeah Coach, that wouldn't be a good-look for you at all."

"Not at all."

Big Browbow gathered the team in the home end zone as was our tradition. Fans still ripping and running around in post celebration of the victory. He put his head down trying to choke back his emotions about the performance of his boys. He began his post-game speech and in the backdrop stood his wife and daughter proudly watching, waiting, for their time to congratulate him.

"Men, I'm proud of all of you…that's right I said *men*, because that is what you are… I watched you all grow up tonight, right here on this field. This was a great night for the Southside High Warriors, but also sad, because two of our Warriors are not with us, as we said before the game, let's not forget them, let's not forget Isum and Yosef both who are seniors this year…join hands and let us pray for them tonight."

From a distance, you could see several Rayen players and coaches jogging towards us to join in the after-game prayer. We all bowed our heads.

"After this manner therefore pray ye: Our Father which art in heaven, Hallowed be thy name. Thy kingdom come, Thy will be done in earth, as it is in heaven. Give us this day our daily bread and forgive us our debts, as we forgive our debtors and lead us not into temptation, but deliver us from evil: For thine is the kingdom, and the power, and the glory, forever. Amen."

I felt every word Coach Browbow spoke, I kept my head bowed and continued in prayer for the two boys, but especially for Isum, because he still had life in his body and a chance to live and not return to his vomit. He was the one that I wanted to save and I would use Hutch Campbell to help me do it.

Standing in the ruins
Of another Black man's life,
Or flying through the valley
Separating day and night.
"I am death, "cried the Vulture,
"For the people of the light.

- Gil Scott Heron

16

DA-BOX

I STAYED AROUND long after the crowd left. I wanted to catch Coach B alone to talk to him. I leaned against an old gray metal linked fence and watched Mr. Hall shut down each light one by one. There was a misty haze right above the scoreboard and it gave me a nervous feeling from my past.

As I entered the coaches office Mrs. B and Marva were there, so I told Coach that I would come back another time or maybe we could talk later when he was alone.

"No Coach, it's cool, what's up," he said with a smile.

"Coach, can Marva be excused from this conversation?" I asked.

"Wait outside girl… me and your mother will be out shortly."

"Yes sir," she quietly exited.

"What's on your mind Coach, by the way, you called a great game tonight."

"Preciate that… just stuck to the game plan… yeah-aahhh, I wanted to talk with you real quick about Isum, not so much about him but more about what he told me."

"What he told you-told you what?"

Big Browbow's face went from happy to serious in a seconds time. He sat down on the edge of his desk folded his arms and waited to hear what I was going to say next. His wife edged up in the large coaching chair still being as lady-like as possible but also with an attentive ear.

"Well Coach… he said that Yosef told him, that you and Mrs. B were yelling at Yosef the night he died… and…well… it made me think to ask you about that night…if Yosef said anything that could be a clue to his state of mind before he left out of here. Because according to Isum, he said that Yosef was crying and really upset…and Yosef's grandparents are still struggling with answers to what happened. Coach,

I'm not saying that you have any answers, but I'm hoping you do so I can tell them something."

Mrs. B quickly stood up from the chair she so delicately sat in and rushed toward him to stop his possible revelation. She positioned herself at the front of the desk next to her husband and before he could respond, she did. Big Browbow's head dropping quickly because he knew she was about to go into black woman diva mode.

"First of all, let me say this to you, anything that happens with my child is our business and no one else's, especially some damn Isum Duart. Furthermore, Mr. Jones, Yosef may he rest in peace, he wasn't any good for my daughter. I liked him. I'd be lying to say that I didn't, my husband obviously liked him, hell- she loved him, but this is high school, and we want the best for her and even though he was good at football and a good student. I never saw him as anything more than a high school boyfriend for her and then she ends up… so embarrassing, turned my child into some type of whore," she went back to the chair and crossed her legs and folded her arms in a disgusted position.

My thoughts going back to when I hid behind that couch when I first heard that word "whore" and the ugly meaning it held.

Big Browbow covers her emotion-riddled words with composure and admittance.

"What's done is done, let it rest, they both were wrong for having sex and carrying on like they did. Both of them are good kids and made mistakes, but so did I-we- at that age too baby. When he left here Anthony he was fine, other than being upset- because we did yell at him, but he knew exactly why we were yelling at him," he said.

Mother Browbow stood up again with the quickness of a teenager.

"And if he was acting funny or strange or whatever after he left us, it was probably because he and his buddy- Isum- were probably high on something. Everybody in the school knows that all these boys do is smoke boy, it ain't no secret and that goes for the football team too. And you know like they say Coach, 'birds of a feather…" Mrs. Browbow accused angrily but continued her rant. "Yosef was not about to destroy my daughter's future, with-some demon-seed baby, they not married and wasn't about to get married. I feel bad for his grandparents, I feel bad that he is dead, Antietam, I feel bad for you, but I wanted to kill both of them after all this…this… so-called relationship fell into my lap.

How does that make my husband look… and you too, you helped raise the boy… is that what you taught him COACH… to have sex with any girl who would give it up, cause I'm sure Marva wasn't the first?" Big Browbow put his hand in front of her giving the motion to back off and stop chastising me as if I was her child.

I looked at her with contempt and slowly turned with a disgusted scoff on my face and walked away. I decided that I would never look at the Browbow family the same again; especially Coach B for letting his wife say those things about Yosef.

I left the locker room walking out into total darkness except for the one light that Mr. Hall left on waiting for us all to leave.

"Take it easy Coach," Mr. Hall said.

"You to Mr. Hall," he replied while reaching in his pocket to grab his car keys.

"Uh-Coach, before you leave…I know that no one pays any attention me 'round here.

You know I am just the custodian, to most folks I may as well be a slave and I done kept my mouth shut for over a year now, except for me telling the cops how I found Yosef that morning. If you remember that morning Coach, before all of you arrived, it was just me here, and Yosef lying under those bleachers.

I can say this much I don't think he fell by no accident. That woman in there-Mrs. Browbow, she is an evil woman Coach. I hear many things-done heard a lot of things these past 37 years I been working here, and that night that Yosef and that young girl was up in those bleachers talking… Mrs. Browbow was furious, she screamed for that girl to come out of those bleachers with a fury I never seen nor heard in my life, especially coming from a sanctified woman.

Now-Coach don't get me wrong I ain't saying what you may think I'm saying, but she was mad enough to kill. That girl ran out of those bleachers and jumped in the car and they drove off. I told Yosef that I had to lock up and that he had to go home. He looked at me with the saddest face you could imagine. The rain was coming down so hard that night. Coach I watched him come down from those bleachers and walk out that gate. I shut it all down and I went home and the next morning when I returned is when I saw him right there-dead."

Mr. Hall's words penetrated my brain like a needle. He meant well. I figured that he had been holding onto words for a year that finally burned through him like a lit match in someone's pocket. His face and hands were aged, from years of work, I imagine. The things he has probably seen all these years I am sure could fill up the pages of ten novels.

I got into my black Acura truck, turned on my favorite GZA song from 1995 and sat for a moment recollecting times when this stadium looked better, the grass stayed greener and groomed. How the booster club pumped money into the program but now, they were just dusty pictures on a wall living in perpetual honor of autumns gone by. I wished I could rewind time so that the players could enjoy the benefits of a supported program. Instead, they got left with leaking ass ceilings, rusty running water, poor equipment, and ungrateful parents and fence standers whose careers mounted to nothing.

I cozied up in the driver's seat, shifted to D and began the drive down out of the parking lot onto the street. I drove past the home-bleachers where Yosef died. I became sad. Fogg began to settle over the stadium and in the distance; I could see the shadows of that last steel mill. I stopped and back up, and rolled down the passenger side window and looked at the makeshift memorial that was set up for Yosef at the spot of his death.

I could see that over a year's time Yosef's friends and loved ones tried to keep it updated with candles, bears and different mementoes, but the weather had tarnished the colors, thinned the fabrics and blown most of it deep down into the bushes of the L. I made the decision to clean up the sacred place that people made for Yosef. I walked back to the locker room and got a flashlight and a box from Mr. Hall's office to put all the things that had become part of the trash of the L, in an attempt to separate the good intentions from the evil ones, both, which shared the same ground.

The flashlight shined through the dense half dead brush and I could see liter of all types that had attached itself to the trees and small shrubs like paper leaves. You could hear the scurrying clacking sound of high-heels running like mice out of the darkness, thinking that I was the police coming to make a bust. The farther in I walked, the dirtier and more unbelievable it became, the flashlight grasping images of crack vials and used condoms scattered on the ground. An old stained mattress almost out of sight of any unsuspecting eye, except for maybe a stray dog laid pushed far into the darkness. I wondered about the men and women who laid down on it together to turn a trick. I wondered how it became so bad that the perils of loneliness could make a person live this way.

I picked up a small wooden cross that now leaned over into the mud and put it in the box. There was sun faded photos of Yosef with a spectrum of bleeding colors, and wet ripped open teddy bears toppled over one another and candles of different colors, some standing erect and some knocked down. The box was now nearly full. I had enough for one night and would maybe come back at a better time during better weather. I began my walk back out the brush, ducking under protruding branches continuing to step over ghetto belongings that were left on the earth for God to clean up. The flashlight swayed side to side as I sidestepped over broken glass, that is when I saw a water bottle, a Southside High Football water bottle that we use for practice which immediately made him mad. *"No wonder we never have enough bottles for the team, these kids act like it's their own personal container, and one of these dummies just tossed it down here with the rest of the trash, well maybe I shouldn't assume the worst, it could have been a part of the memorial for Yosef,"* I said aloud.

I added it to the box. As I walked to the back of my truck I looked inside, seeing all the things collected, a wooden cross, tattered bears, faded photo's, dead flowers, ink bled hand written letters, candles and a water bottle. All materials things, but things that people placed there out of love for Yosef. Those things in that box suddenly became special to me, special like my uncles Bible, Vietnam pictures, the old Southside High letter and Yosef's helmet that sits on the mantelpiece at my home. I held the box like it was more than just trash or blown away objects downcast at the end of some guttered out street. I made space for it. I moved my practice clothes and playbooks to one side. I loaded it into my truck that had now taken on a holy importance in my soul. Initially, I thought about taking it home, but then I decided that tomorrow I would take it to Coach Browbow's office and let him decide what to do with it.

"Let all things be done properly and in order," I thought in my head.

Women been leading the way, since Roxanne Shante
And the Unit had Flava and Jay had Marcy neighbors that waved
Lookin' confused, I be like "Cool, maybe it's age"
When I see afro puffs, I think maybe it's Rage

- Rapsody

17

MAR & RA

MONDAY MORNING CAME quicker than usual or maybe that was the way it seemed. I grew uneasy about the box. I wondered what Browbow would want to do with it. Suddenly I found myself rushing around, forgetting this and that, until anxiety steadily closed in on me. I had to stop and breathe. *"Slow down brother,"* I said aloud. I looked over at the prescription bottle of yellow pills feeling the need to grab one and pop it down and keep moving, but today I wanted to use my mind to sedate my nervousness.

I decided to walk to school again carrying the brown box under my right arm. The morning was quiet. It seemed as if the entire neighborhood took a sigh of relief seeing that the big game was over and the thought of Yosef's death was-sealed for a solid year now. I was unsure of what to think, or say to Browbow's and his wife when I saw them, but I knew I could not avoid them, so I prepared my mind for that encounter regardless of when it happened.

As I came within reach of the entrance to the school, I stopped to talk to Officer Jameson who was at his usual post.

"Your boy played good Friday night," I said.

"Thanks bro', he did a nice job out there, jus like his pops-huh?" Jameson replied.

"No doubt man, you were a baller."

"Yeah we had a nice team back then, but still, I shoulda been the starting tail-back, but I will give you your props Ant' you was nice QB."

I laughed. "I don't know about the starter… but you had a great career as a receiver so we both did our thing out there."

"True, but you had the favor of the coach, that man-Coach Edwards-loved you, treated you like the golden boy… but any way bro', good game last night."

"You hear ya'self- Walt? I asked him.

"What you talking about man, of course I hear myself, what I just said was the truth and you know it."

"I say that because you sittin' up here blowin' down on me and how Edwards treated me and you tell me every damn day that Walt Jr. should be carrying us… you know what's that called don't you?" I asked.

"Yeah I know what it's called, and I ain't being no hypocrite, that shit back when we played was different, now man with this internet shit and all these camps and scouting combines, it's all about exposure and he can't get that fuckin' 'round with your play callin'."

Jameson shook his head with a stupid look on his face. A look that I had grown used to seeing from him over the years, he was still holding on to high school envies and dreams. I walked away not wanting to add to the task already that was laid before me, turning in that box to Coach. *"This dude still talking about high school football days… I feel bad for his son having to hear his mouth before-after and during the game."* I thought as I headed to Browbow's office and hoped to be able to leave it there with him.

The secretary Ms. Jorge greeted me with a smile.

"Morning Coach." she said.

"Morning Mrs. J."

"How you feeling after the big game Coach, kids were into it, the boys played hard out there. I was so excited."

"I feel good, tired, but good."

"Are you here to see the boss?" She asked.

"Yes."

"Is he expecting you?"

"No, but it's important."

"Okay, let me go back and see if he can see you right now."

Despite how cool she was, she always did her job and I couldn't be mad at her for that. I stood there for a few minutes as students came in and out of the office for late slips, to drop off money, and just to say hello to the huddle of adults who hung out there each morning.

"You can go back now Coach."

"Thanks."

"What up's Coach, I want to show you something before I head to my room," I said, holding the box in my hands.

"What you got?" he asked.

"I was headed home on Friday after our talk and as I drove down Delason. I was looking at that memorial that the people in the community made for Yosef, you know, at the place where he died-under the bleachers. Most of it blew down the L, so I went and tried to clean it up as best I could. I wasn't sure what to do with it all. I didn't want to throw it away, so I brought it to you."

"Boy Antietam you somethin' else… you actually climbed into those bushes with all that garbage, and I mean that literally… do you think his grandparents would want any of it," he asked me.

"Nah-they… they… I don't think so and if they did I ain't taking it over there, can't take the way his grandmother looks at me with her heartbroken eyes."

"I definitely understand that… let me take a peek." He walked his fingers through the box skimming to see what was there.

"We can leave it here until I figure out exactly what to do with it all, but I know I just don't want to throw it away either it's been made into trash once and we not gonna make it into trash twice that's for damn sure. Put it in that storage closet over there. Just set it down on top of those other boxes, it will be safe, and Antietam…make sure you see my wife before you leave today, she has a few things she wants to say to you, okay?"

"Yes, sir," I said as I walked out towards my room.

***

As soon my class began, the questions immediately follow to start each day.

"Coach J', is the world going to end?" asked Andre Stubbs, one of the brighter students.

I liked questions like this, it gave me the chance to teach what was taught to me, but gotta be careful with my answers as not to cross the line of what teachers were allowed to discuss with students.

"Andre, let me put it to you like this, the world was made to be inhabited forever, but to really answer your question, yes-the world will be destroyed and two-thirds of the people will be destroyed with it… now you do the math from there, who is left?"

"So that means that one-third will be left right?" Andre answered and asked at the same time.

"Yes, that's right, but let me ask you another question, if the world will be destroyed then why are-one-third of the people going to still be alive, shouldn't all people be destroyed?"

"Dang Coach, that's a good question, I don't know that answer to that one."

By this time, the entire class's attention focused on me waiting for the answer.

"Well, what does the word world mean? The world does not always refer to the earth. It can also refer to a time, or people, like the world of sports etc… so when that time comes, the earth will still be here but two-thirds of people will be destroyed for their evil and some will stay here because of their good… thus the mathematical equation of the thirds. The question is which third will you be in Andre?"

"The good one I hope," he replied.

"I hope that I will be too…"

A soft knock at the door broke the question and answer segment of the conversation. It was Marva. She had a humble embarrassed look on her face. I stepped out into the hallway to talk with her.

"Coach, I wanted to apologize for what my mother said to you the other day. I heard the whole thing and I wanted to say sorry about what she said. I loved Yosef and a lot has happened since that day he died, stuff that I have regrets about. He talked about you all the time, Coach said this or Coach said that, he really looked up to you. When he died, I wanted to come and see how you were doing, but I never did, I should have, because I know you miss him as much as I do and Yosef would have wanted me to check up on you, so I'm checking now."

"It's okay, you don't have to apologize for them 'Mar', they are supposed to protect you and defend you. And Yosef spoke of you all the time too, he used to ask me would I come to yalls wedding when that day came… and you know that I told him I would have. Your parents are good people and you're lucky to have them, think about some of the kids you go to school with, some ain't got parents or even grandparents for that matter that actually care about them, but at least Yosef had me and you, and his grandparents."

"Coach, did he ever talk to you about his mom and dad?" Marva asked.

"You know what Marva he did. He told me one time that he wished he could talk with them, he used to always say that he wanted the answer to one question- why they had to give him up to his grandparents, but that was about it, it was quick and to the point," I said to her.

"Oh-okay, I was just wondering. I used to ask him about them but he never would talk about it, said he didn't care what they were doing. He said his father was some type drug dealer and that he hated him. Well, I gotta go to class, again sorry for my mother, sometimes she goes too far," she said as she turned and walked away.

As she walked, you could see Raquel waiting at the end of the hallway.

"What did he say girl," I heard Raquel ask as if she was about to take in some hot gossip. "He said he understood, and that it was cool, but I know it's not, Coach is just being nice."

"Yeah he is," Marva said.

The two friends headed toward the lunchroom to sit in their usual spot to chill and be away from all the cliques of the cafeteria. Raquel was just as pretty and smart as Marva, but had no interest in cheerleading or sports, her focus was on words, she loved words, writing them in a story, journal and in poems. She wrote down almost everything she heard that sounded paper and pen worthy. All of her teachers thought that she could be a journalist if she put her mind to it. She thought so too, but she also thought that her teachers made going to college sound so simple, when she knew that her family struggled to keep the lights on and had no way of paying for a colleg education.

***

Raquel felt the need to protect her friend. Marva had been through so much over the past year, she knew about the pregnancy and about how her parents grew a disliking toward Yosef but lied to everybody about it. Raquel made Marva tell her parents about the baby and made Yosef tell his grandparents. She had a way of getting people to do what she wanted, to tell her things she wanted to find out.

The lunch bell rang and they had to walk past my room to get to their fifth period class. I decided to inquire about a few things for the few minutes that I had. They walked shoulder to shoulder probably to keep whatever they were talking about between them. I stopped them.

"How was lunch, I saw yall in your usual spot, off-in-the-cut." I said.

"Same ole stuff Coach, same ole babes, same ole dudes," Marva said while twisting her wrist.

"Coach, me and Mar' was talking at lunch, will you tell her that Yosef didn't kill himself and that story don't make no-kinda sense at all. Isum Duart is a lying ass-mf!" Raquel exploded in a low voice almost completing the curse.

"I know it don't sound right, but what can I do about it now Ra'?" Marva asked.

"Never said you had to do anything about it, but maybe I found out some shit that will change your mind."

My thoughts held frozen, stopping my need to ask them any questions. The information I was looking for fell right in my lap. So I just sat back and was slow to talk but quick to listen.

"Why do you think Isum is lying," Marva asked as they walked down to the short empty stairwell right next to my door.

"Cause-he is a liar, he lied to me about not having another girl, but he did," she laughed as if it didn't bother her. "After that, his ass has been on my list." She pulls out a small lavender notebook with the title LIARS on it underlined twice.

"See, right there, his ass is number three on my list, one is- my Auntie who lies to me each week about being broke so I can do her hair fo free, and two, is- my little jerk ass brother."

"You actually carry that around with you?" Marva asked laughing.

"You see it don't you, gotta keep track of this type of stuff girl," Raquel replied while letting her hip slip to one side.

Coming down the steps was Jonita Barnes, Shugg Anderson, Chas Dove, Mykayla MK Wallace and another girl who I didn't know.

Jonita and MK were on the cheerleading team but was like Isum in this way, with two sets of friends that were not cheerleaders. That is who Chas and this other girl represented-the other set of friends.

Seeing them together reminded me about the circles I used to run with in high school. I would be a hypocrite to say that I didn't have a not so well-behaved group of dudes I kicked it with…I started off with Robert Bell but migrated to dudes like Deaf-P, Stretch and Blackeye-Pee.

MK she was smart and pretty and had a bright future but only if she stayed away from Jonita. MK grew up on the Eastside until her mother moved to the Southside before she entered seventh grade. She had that Eastside swag that the girls who were native Southside hated about her. Being on the cheerleading team help to ease the image of not from being from this side, but still she had it rough at times. I stayed concerned about her especially since she befriended a girl like Jonita. Jonita led her to Chas and Chas led them all to trouble.

Jonita was a time bomb set to go off at any minute. She had a quick temper and ill-fated words frequently came out her mouth. All five were the gossipers, instigators and meddlers of all types of business that was not theirs-especially Shugg.

Being on the cheerleading team didn't stop Jonita from joining in on the ugly looks the other two girls gave to Marva and Raquel or any other innocent flowered face girl walking down the hallway or entering the ladies restroom…but the real troublemaker out of that bunch was Dove. Dove was smart enough to know just how far to go without getting to trouble. She was the back shoulder instigator but out in front first punch thrower. She was what the Italian mobsters called the muscle of the group, like Machine Gun Kelly or Bishop from the movie Juice.

If a fight was going to go down between Jonita and Marva, the first blows would happen with Chas and Raquel.

Raquel turned to Marva and said, "damn I hate Chas and Jonita is so fake and stupid, she likes Craig Cotton, that niggah from the Northside that been liking you since forever?"

"Yeah he always up in my face, he don't give a fuck about Yosef being dead…he didn't like Yosef and don't like Hutch. Yosef told me that, not sure why but that's what he told me." Marva said.

"That don't surprise me, cause Jonita told me one night when I caught her ass drunk at this party, she starts telling me about you liking Craig and that's why she don't like you…then she starts telling me about who those five boys that was there the night Yosef died. She said it was Craig Cotton, Sonny Reaves, Poompus Staten and the Gaddy brothers."

"Gaddy brothers…I heard about them, but I don't know-em," Marva said.

"Dey ain't nobody-girl, some niggahs that tag-along with Sonny and Craig. So she tells me that dem five niggahs was waiting for Yosef and Hutch that night after the game, but Hutch got a ride home with his father."

"Are you serious?" Marva asked.

"Yeah I'm serious. This chick told me that stupid ass story last week. Sonny is grown. He dropped out of school a long time ago. Craig just follows whatever Sonny does, that his little fuck-boy.

Poompus Staten-he cool most of the time, don't know why he kicks it with them because he is smart, he showed me his report card one day-straight-B's. Now, dem Gaddy brothers, is a whole 'nother story, they grown too. Stacy is a shooter and Rick is the stick up kid.

Marva begins to cry. She covers her face from the other kids coming down into the stairwell. I wanted to intervene but I didn't.

"Don't cry," Raquel said. She reaches in her purse and gives Marva some tissue.

"If Yosef wouldna been talking to my parents that night maybe he could have got a ride with Hutch too and he'd be alive."

"Don't look at it that way Marva, can't think about what-ifs."

"I know…"

"Jonita claims that Walt was there too, but he ran."

"We go to school with some dumb-asses… I hate it around here; I used to really like going here and coming to school, but after what happened to Yosef and all… I just hate it now. My so holier-than-thou mother made me get that abortion and I hate her for that, all these stupid ass-bitches up in here looking at me crazy. Yosef wanted to keep it, he didn't believe in abortions but what choice did I have," Marva said sadly.

"You ain't sure who knows and who don't know. Stop freaking out and being all 'noid about it, as many as these raggedy ass broads up in here that had abortions and don't give a dam about it, at least you care, and I was wondering when you were going to talk to me about it, we girls' and you know I got your back," Raquel said.

"Yeah I know we are, but ain't God gonna get me for doing that?" Marva asked her friend but sounding unsure if she really wanted an answer. Raquel looked straight at her. "Look, I ain't 'bout to speak for God and all that, all I know is, that your parents made you do it and that's the story you should tell God when that day comes…"

"Marva laid her head on Raquel's shoulder for a second and they walked down the stairs to class.

MK walking fast to catch them. I called MK's name. She meekly turned around and walked toward me.

"What's going on with you and Marva, yall used to friends, what happened?" I asked her.

"Nothing really t be honest," she said.

"Well it had to be something."

"I don't know, it just how girls are I guess…do you miss Yosef?" she asked, catching me off guard.

"Yes I do, very much; he was like a little brother to me."

"I miss him too, he was good-peeps."

"The best."

"Marva used to be one of my best friends and I hate the fact that we not cool no more. I'm not sure how to fix it now, maybe it's too late…I hate myself for turning my back on her like I have."

We stood there. I was leaning up against the wall with my hands in my pockets.

"The reason why Yosef was so upset that night was because Marva was pregnant, did you know that? She asked.

"Yes I knew."

"Walter was the one who told Yosef that the baby might be Craig's."

“Why would he say that?”

“Word had got back to Yosef that somebody saw Marva and Craig together one night at a party. I was there, they were just talking from what I could see…everybody knows that Craig likes her, he has since middle school and he would do anything to get her to leave Yosef…even lie about getting her pregnant…that baby was Yosef's.

Me and Marva used to be cool and I have always liked her…Craig started harassing her every day, trying to get her to leave Yosef and be his girlfriend, but Marva would never leave Yosef for Craig Cotton.

“Yosef thought that Marva was messing around with Craig Cotton and Yosef thought the baby was Craig's, I repeated, sounding so stupid as I heard my voice in my ears.

“That night she was trying to explain that to Yosef but he didn't believe her,” MK said.

“How do you know this MK, no one was up there with them that night.”

“I just know,” she walks away.

***

My snooping only caused more confusion than already existed in my brain. Haso dropped the same bomb on me with his revelation of what was going on with Cotton and Marva. If what he said was true, then this shit is about to get ugly, way uglier than I am used.

Either way, all the knowledge I had added up to nothing that was worth driving back over to the Nassy's to tell them. I went back into my room to sit down and catch what was left of any free time before heading out again.

I pulled out the middle drawer of my desk. It looked like a small explosion had went off inside. Pens, papers-some wrinkled and some straight were in disarray from the front of the drawer all the way to the back. I managed to find a light yellow sticky note. I dug out a red pen that worked only after trying three other ones that left transparent words on a scrap piece of paper. I blew the dust off the tips of my fingers, along with the accidental black hairs that ended up in that corners of that drawer with all the other whatnots.

I jotted down every clue that I had in my possession. I made a list in no particular order but I wanted to see what I had so far.

1. Suicide (maybe)
2. Killed (maybe)
3. Accident (probably)
4. Jealous Acquaintances (yes)
5. Girls (always)
6. Crooked cops (not sure)
7. Angry cop (yes)
8. Cover up (doubt it)
9. Mrs. Browbow (I hope not)

I watch all the latest detective shows, the old ones too and I wasn't sure if writing down clues on a raggedy ass sticky note was a good practice but I really didn't know where to start. I folded up the small square paper, and shoved it into my pocket and headed down the hall.

Welcome to the Jungle where the cat loves to scratch, the rat squeals
And the polar bear feasts on the blubber of seals
The pack of wolves be scheming on a bunch of gazelles
Where the leopards grab the wildebeest down by its tail

\- GZA JUSTICE

18

ROOM 274

I STOOD IN front of the pop machine in the cafeteria during my lunch duty thinking about what Marva and Raquel talked about. *"Lunch period never changes, still filled with cliques, the athletes sit there, the corner-boys sit there, the quiet kids over there, same shit when I was in school,"* I thought on top of that thought.

The tardy bell sounded off its' last ring, students hurried out of the lunchroom to class. I waited until the last student was out and inserted four quarters into the machine and dropped down a Ginger Ale. I pulled back the tab and took a long swig until I felt a burn in my chest. With each swig I was reminded of my uncle when I would watch him drink Hennessey. At that time, I didn't know what exactly he was sipping on but he seemed to like it, even though he acted to be in pain when he drank it.

I wanted to do things like him because I loved him and wished he was my real father. One day I asked him could I have a drink and he said that I could. So, when he poured himself a shot of his best brown, he poured a young Antietam a shot too. Before you pass judgement on him, let me finish the story. My uncle was not crazy enough to fill me up with strong drink. The hand is quicker than the eye. He was a large man and his frame would block my vision of what he poured into my glass. He handed me my glass and down it went with my young chest catching fire from the burning liquid that I swallowed. In my glass was Ginger Ale Soda. He got me with that sleight of hand trick for years.

My uncle was the greatest of all men that I knew back then and still to this day. He passed away in his sleep my sophomore in college. That day changed me forever.

***

I threw the last drop down. I pushed in the remaining cafeteria chairs and decided to go clear the air and go talk to Mrs. B. I stuck my head in her door, looked from side-to-side, saw that no one was there, and walked toward her desk. I grabbed an index card and decided to leave her a message. I reached over and took a pen from a mug full of pens and pencils. I wrote: Mrs. B, -stopped by to talk, will catch you later today… thanks Coach Jones.

Mrs. B's was room 274 in the science wing. There is much to learn in a class like this. So much information to be taken in within the walls, enough, even for the most hard to reach student that maybe cutting open a frog could spark a slight interest in them.

Marble counter tops aligned the far walls in a ninety-degree angle. Glass jars filled with embryos bathing in embalming fluid sat aligned in a row. Four life size skeletons stood like graveyard guards in each corner of the room. Along the walls were posters of great African American Scientist, George Washington Carver, Katherine Johnson, Ernest Everett Just, Alice Ball and St. Elmo Brady.

Six sinks on three islands took up the middle of the room, which is where the students sat on three-foot swivel stools.

I returned the pen back to its place and stuck the card on the seat of her chair. My eyes caught a picture in a silver frame, a picture of Marva and Yosef, her in her cheerleading uniform and he in his football. The picture confused me. I couldn't make sense of it after hearing the things she said about Yosef last Friday night. But through that confusion, seeing that picture made me smile.

"Coach!" a startled Mrs. Browbow said as she walked in the room.

"Aaay Mrs. B, I replied. "I just left you a note."

"What does it say?" she asked me.

"Nothing really, just that I wanted to talk to you about last Friday."

"Listen, Marva been up and down on my case about the things I said to you and some of the things I said, I meant, but my tone was all wrong. I just want the best for my child and I'm a mother so I went into protect mode, but I should not have spoken to you like that or about Yosef like that either, I was waaaaay out of line."

"It's okay, I understand, but it sorta caught me off guard that's all."

"Again Coach, I apologize."

"Plant Bio time again huh- Mrs. B?" I asked changing the subject

"Yes, I spent the first few months covering the vascular make up of plants and this month plant secretions," she replied.

I looked into a small glass greenhouse that she kept locked to keep any curious students' hands away from the delicate but unsafe plants. There were three plants growing in separate containers. All three looking similar to the weeds that grew in my yard but I knew it couldn't be that simple.

"That's our student greenhouse Coach, but I'm the only one that can access this particular one, these are the toxic plants that have to be maintained by an adult. In the past, I could leave this unlocked, but that was before a student reached in there and destroyed everything. So now... with these mischievous kids, it's under lock and key, all I need is for one of them to do something dumb, and there goes my job, but anyway I know you're short on time, but if you want to learn more before you go, each one has a label that gives a good explanation."

"Oh, okay," I began to read each one aloud.

"So, from what I read my question is- are all these plants related somehow?" I asked her.

"Yes they are, good job Coach you sound like you have some scientist in you, I wish my students could pick up on information that fast," she replied.

"I wish they could too, especially some of the football players. And while we on that, how are they doing in here?" I asked.

"Fine, just fine, a few of them struggle from time to time but they know that you or my husband will be up in here so fast that they stay on top of those grades struggling or not."

"I wish they would have had this class when I was in this school, all we had back then were the basics, nothing like the stuff you teach," I said.

"Well, that-back then-wasn't that long ago," she laughed. "But you know how kids are these days, on their phones, some of them are asleep or daydreaming and the others are trying their best to pay attention with all the chaos that those others do every single day.

However, it does help to have something to look at and touch like the plants, and animals to dissect along with all the other displays… teaching has changed so much over the years, kids need more ways to be reached today. You know what I mean, our children are very needy and it gets harder each year to teach them."

We both laughed.

"Where are your class books and what chapter are these plants in, the ones in the greenhouse I just read about?" I asked, as I looked over at the bookshelf that was full of a variety of science books.

"Don't use those text books, go to my desk and use my teachers' edition, it's up there somewhere and the page is bookmarked, oh' and please ignore the ripped page that some ill-behaved student tore from my book and of course it's the page with the lesson plan on it and the whole chapter breakdown."

I picked up the book and quickly looked it over. I could see the torn out page that she was referring too. I flipped through a few more pages skimming for eye-catching facts.

"I been teaching this lesson for so many years that I really don't need that missing page, but it still pisses me off that our children feel the need to be destructive to information that is for their use and benefit.

The adults appreciate what I have to offer more than most of my students. Teachers loiter in here all the time, just like you are doing right now. I guess most of them hoping to catch us dissecting a frog or maybe they think we are making a witch's potion in big black vat.

"I have had parents stop in, board members, hell, Officer Jameson even brought his silly self-up here, asking can he cut up a frog," she said.

"Dang, I guess people are curious about science, you-know-how things work and grow,"

> "I guess," shrugging her shoulders. "Don't find to many Black people who take to science and math, it scares our kids away, thus why we are always last in anything that has to do with the two, last in test scores, last in the state report card… just last, last, last, she said.

"Well, let me get back to my room before the bell rings and these halls get crowded up. Thanks again Mrs. B for taking a minute to talk."

"We are family, right?" she asked me.

With a smile, I answered. "Yes ma'am." That question made me feel better about the Browbow family again.

He ended up on the block with kid scooters and ice cream, put in and out of foster homes, until he was 19, stealing for food and didn't do for enjoyment, at the time of lay off, shut down and unemployment.
He moved into a new world, to seek his fortune.
And suited himself to the times with extortions.
A hustle that was ruled by men and murder,
He earned enough for his daily bread and wanted to move further.
He knew no good, could come from such a sin
Had issues as a kid, so he held it all within.
And he pursued the game so hotly, on a path of destruction. Even though the road was rocky
Very caught up in his own drive for dominance
And to know that he would pay in the end was common sense, some say he had a long deserved death, and then he felt relieved when they were told he left.

- GZA JUSTICE

19

ISUM DUART II

I'M BACK AT the Happening House Juvenile Facility, but this time with Hutch Campbell and Raquel.

"How can I help you?"

"Uh-we here to see Isum-Isum Duart," Hutch said.

"Arms out, turn around, go up to the front desk and get checked in."

"Okay," I said.

"You have an ID?" the guard asked Raquel and Hutch.

"Yeah we do."

"Let me see if ya'll on his visitors list…Boyd…aaannnnnd…Campbell...walk up to the door and I'll buzz of yall in. What's up Coach, how you been?" The guard asked me.

"I'm good brotha-I'm good, just making my rounds checking on my boy." I said.

"This place is crazy," Hutch said aloud. "They got my man locked up in here like he an animal or something."

Hutch and Raquel walked into the muted painted room and sat down at the last table to wait for Isum to come out. It was just after dinner and you could smell the poorly cooked food that lingered in the air.

Isum walked around the corner dressed in county orange, a pair of flimsy flip-flops and dirty white socks. His hair had grown out high and woolly, which for him wasn't a bad look cause it was the latest style on the street.

"What up kid?" Hutch slid his chair up closer to the table. "You-good?"

Isum looked weary like he hadn't slept in a minute.

"I'm just in here maintainin' as best I can. I be trying to stay out the way but dudes be testin' you up in here. They got all types of niggahs in here, some from Cleveland, Dayton, Columbus, so you know they think they gotta rep dey city. Me and a dude from Cleveland got into a back and forth about who plays better football, of course I said we do. This dude started gettin' all serious actin' like he wanted some minutes in the ring, so ya'll know me, I was like-what's up? Then the guards jumped all between us… all that shit over some football so you know if it was over some money, a niggah might be dead up in here."

"Man you need to chill-that-shit-out. You gon get time added to what you already gone get," Hutch said.

"Man, I be trying to mind my business, but shit is hetic in here, nothing sweet about this place. Gotta stay alert at all times."

"Have you talked to a lawyer yet?"

"Yeah, he ain't shit, told me to take a plea. I wish I could dump him but the judge appointed him to me. One dude in here told me that they gone make me wait until I turn eighteen and they gonna send me up, man-I'm looking at three to five years bro."

"How he know what they tryin' to do, he locked up wit' you," Raquel asked.

"That's what I asked him, that same question, he said he been locked up so many times in juvie that he knows the game."

"I guess, all yall some dumb-asses if you ask me," she replied shaking her head.

"Why you bring her with you?" Isum asked Hutch as he pointed his finger in her face.

"Why you put me on your visitor's list clown? Raquel asked as her neck rotated around.

"Oh yeah, I did didn't I? I musta been trippin' when I did that dumb shit, especially since you out here sayin' that I got somethin' to do with Yosef's death. Yeah you doing all that chit-chattering Ra' but you stay not likin' a niggah but you up here all in my face."

My eyes immediately closed because this basic conversation was about to turn into a gangsta rap video.

"First of all, I never said that, all I said is-that the shit don't make sense and maybe you know more than you tellin', because I know more than Ima tell you and I really don't care if you mad or whatever, I came up here to show you some love boy. You act like a little-bitch sometimes Isum fo-real."

Hutch jumps in the mix. "The news was talking about the case again last week. The reporter was up at practice talking to Coach B. He talked about the team having a legit shot at the playoffs, but then it went back to the stuff about Yosef's death being a cold case and you being locked up in here.

"Bout what…about me havin' something' to do with Yu's death, what did he say about me man, I know that fat mug sold me out, didn't he?" Isum said.

"Naw-man, you know how Coach do it, he was all political, he said that you were a good kid and player but came from a troubled background, but never gave him any problems and that he was shocked about went on that night Yosef died.

Isum laughed.

"But why did he have to say that I come from a bad background, everybody don't need to know all that shit," Isum said.

"I don't know-sound better to the news I guess," chimed Raquel.

"Yosef's grandparents got interviewed today too, they wanna blame somebody. I just hope it aint you," Hutched confessed to his friend.

"Blame me? I ain't do-shit man-I had love for him, just like I got love for you. I told you the truth already man. Me and Walt left him up in the bleachers! Coach Jones was just up here last week and I told the whole story to him, the whole thing, stuff I didn't tell my dumb-ass lawyer. Didn't I Coach?"

"Why not man, that don't make sense, why wouldn't you tell your lawyer the story, so it can be over, that is his job to prove that you innocent ain't it?" Hutch curiously asked.

"Cause he's a dumb-ass," Raquel jabbed.

"Yosef told me not to bro', so I didn't. You know how we get down, like I told Coach, Yosef was in Big Browbow's office and whatnot, and they was going off on him about all types of shit."

"Shit like what Isum, damn man stop playing-this ain't no game man, you bout to get some time over this shit!" Hutch said angrily.

Isum pointed at Raquel. "She knows, don't you Ra?" Your boy knocked Marva up man, that type of shit. Before you even ask me bro' only-me-you-them and Coach Jones know about this shit, so please man-stay on the hush with this one…on Yosef man." Isum held his hand out for their secret dap-shake to solidify their bond of promise.

"No doubt…on Yosef."

Now, Hutch knew better in his mind than to put anything on a dead person. He knew that those types of dealings, was be considered idol worship according to the truth from the lessons that I taught him.

"Damn man, damn."

"Yeah it's a lot deeper than people know," Isum said.

"When we walked out of there he was upset, like for-real, we both done seen him mad before, but this time was different, he was talking but not to us, he had his head phones blasting and just kept pounding his fist into his hand. Then he just stopped-went back and got Marva, and we headed down the L and then we saw them N-words. You thought I was going to say niggahs didn't you Coach?"

"You just said it," I said smiling.

We both laughed for a second. That quickening lesson taught by their coach-me. All lessons made up about meaningless words that loom so large in the black community, words like niggah, bitch and hoe.

"Did you ask him about Marva? What did he say-she said about it? Hutch asked.

"All he said was that he was scared."

"What about this gun?" Raquel asked. "And what about Sonny Reaves and dem?"

Isum's eye's rolling to the celling. "Who is dem Raquel-damn?" Isum asked at the same time making fun of her overly street slang.

"Dem-is the Ready-Rock-Boys, that's who dem is!" she yelled back haulting his sarcasm. "And you say dem all the time boy, so stop frontin' like you-some-typa-proper-talking-up-town typa dude."

"I don't roll with them, they just know me and I just know them, you know who I get down with Raquel, growing up in da-YO, man dudes started getting shot in the streets because of drugs, girls, hoods all that." Hutch nodded in agreement.

"Man we had to protect ourselves. Yall know we not shooting nobody out here especially Yosef, but somebody was always talkin' shit to him about football and that shit started botherin' him cause they was makin' it seem like he thought he was better than everybody else and yall know jealousy out here in these streets equals a dude gettin' killed.

He even knew that Walt pops ain't like him even though him and Walt are cool. He would tell me about it when we would be getting dressed for practice. I told him that we can't get caught slippin' out here so I coped a gun. At first, he was like nah-man I don't fool with guns, but one day he just asked me for it and I gave it to him. So we just hid it in a bag or whatever we had to put it in. Yall know how it is walking home after a game passing through the L that shit be scary man, all types of dudes and dope fiends be hanging out over there especially after a game, and on that night it was raining all hard and still then nigg' –I mean-them dudes was out there.

"So yall was just sharing a gun like it was a toy? Hutch asked, as he rested his hands on top of his head.

"Yeah, I know it sounds crazy but-ay-it's crazy out here ain't it? Sometimes he had it. Sometimes I did. On that night, I went and got it from him, because like I told Coach J I wasn't going to no damn Eastside after the game without that gun, I don't care what nobody say...so before we got ready for the game he gave it back to me right there in the locker room.

When we left out that night, we was ready to make that walk home, so I put the gun in my backpack and didn't bring it back out until all that shit jumped off. That's the only reason I had that gun on me that night and now, I'm glad I did 'cause if Yosef woulda had it, he wouldna even pulled it out and if he did, he wouldna shot it and I might be dead too. I know that might sound like I don't give a fuck about him, but man I thought I was gonna die that night. I'm tellin' yall the real-help me man," Isum pleaded.

"Help you, how bro, I don't know shit other than what you just told me and I don't know anybody wit' any pull that can help you. The only person I can even ask for help is Coach J' and he ain't no lawyer Isum, he just a football coach. No offense Coach," Hutch said to me.

"Man, I know he ain't no lawyer, but damn man can yall at least try to get Yosef's grandparents to chill-the-fuck-out, Coach go talk to them for me… please man."

All eyes were on me, all of them waiting for me to give an answer to Isum's request.

"Aight Isum, I can do that. I will talk with them for you but that's all I can do is ask."

"Cool," Isum replied.

Hutch and Isum gave a final dap and a brotherly hug to one another. Raquel feeling the love wrapped her arms around both of them and gave a hard squeeze. Isum's face lit up with affection and calmness from her touch.

Tryin to paint a perfect picture and excel
In case you didn't know
Never movin' backwards
Complicated
Know what I mean?

- Rakim

20

STAY THE COURSE

THE NEXT DAY at practice.

There were two games left and if we were victorious then we would make the playoffs. Right now, we sat at spot number nine and in the state of Ohio only the top eight teams advance. We had defeated Wilson game eight. Our last two games where against North Heights and Victory.

"These last two weeks have to be on point," I said to Lovelady the wide receiver coach. "I got you, we'll be ready," he said as he tossed the red dummy bags into place.

The closer the playoffs get the more bystanders come to practice to watch the team and show their support and of course to share their criticism. It was an exciting time to be a Southside Warrior. *We gotta' keep the kids focused*, I thought. Parents, girlfriends and star struck youths all dangled on the fence or sat in the bleachers closely watching their favorite players. Some were there just to socialize and hangout.

Hutch and the other quarterbacks were warming up with the running backs, they were working on play timing and handoffs. Walter Jr. and Hutch were in group-one and Greg Brown and Wendal Stewart ran in group-two.

"Reps guys-we gotta get reps." I stressed. "Can't have any fumbles or mental mistakes, it only gets harder from here," I said as I clapped my hands.

"We got this Coach, let's go yall," Hutch yelled loudly across the field. He was a good captain. He took it serious like it was a job, but his payment was a chocolate milk and cheese sandwich from the lunchroom, but even with that small token, he made the most of his title. He wanted to be the best. Things he had learned in little league, things like leadership and competition, but the main thing was love,

love from coaches to players and how important that can be, that thing that Yosef and I shared.

He knew, like many of the kids on the team did, that they were loved by the adults who coached them. They were cared for by us, if they needed food they got fed, if they needed a ride home, they got one. If a single parent whether man or woman had the lights or heat turned off due to an unpaid bill, the coaches would anti-up and pay it. All those things were a part of our program.

The whistle blew; the team hustled to the next drill. This was Walter's favorite part of practice, INSIDE RUN! "Let's go O-line, let's go- DOGGS," he yelled high-fiving each one of them as they lined for the drill.

Coach Greene rallied up seven scout defenders to go seven on seven versus the starters. "If you not gonna go hard versus the first team, them don't come out here, we don't need you," yelled Greene.

Coach Depriest, the youngest coach on the staff was the offensive line coach. He stayed fired up and expected that same fire from his group. He did his daily taunting of the scout defense. "Ya'll bout to get the *Big DOOOGGG* treatment," everyone would laugh. Practice was timely and polished. We were locked in and ready to play out the rest of the season.

***

We breezed past the last two opponents and finished the year with an 8-2 record just enough to get the last playoff spot in Division 2-Region 6. We were the 2006 City League Champions and Coach Browbow was the City Series League Coach of the Year.

I printed out the region 6 playoff bracket, spot 8 matched you up with mathematically against the number 1 ranked team in your region, one versus eight, two versus seven and so on. Our opponent was the Red Castle Demons, they had been to the state playoffs for the last ten years, and made the final four twice.

On paper we were outmatched. We knew it in real life too. They were bigger and faster and their best players were better than ours with the exception of Hutch. The experience that we didn't have showed on almost every play that we tried to execute. Red Castle was steady and consistent with their game plan while we tousled around like an anthill that was compromised by an aardvark.

Each quarter seemed to take forever because of the physical pounding we were receiving.

We fought hard, but got outplayed at every level and aspect of the game except at Quarterback. Hutch put on a one-man show but he couldn't do enough to beat them by himself. The game ended in a blowout.

Head coaches have speeches imbedded in their memories for times of great wins and heartbreaking loses. Browbow was no different in that characteristic, but the words he spoke were fatherly, he spoke to them like sons and not just athletes at a school.

He stood in silence in front of his team surrounded by his coaches. He wanted to make sure as to say the right words, because these were the moments that players remember forever. He looked down at Hutch who had tears in his eyes.

Sometimes depending on how big the loss was, or better said, how a team lost, it can cause splinters, splinters of doubt that seep into the heads of players. They can't pull themselves together after a defeat, they can't take a knee within the tightness of the team. They remain on the outskirts of the inner circle after games but during a win, they are the nearest to the front of the group, eyes up and attentive on the coaches words-all because in victory it is easy to stay as one.

Browbow looked over at Jerome Robinson, a kid who only played one year but was one of the hardest workers we had on the team that season-he was intact. Free safety Toni Jackson laid on his back with his hands over eyes trying to hide his pain-he was down but he intact. Then there was Henderson, Clark, Nolan and Jacobs all not on a knee, standing off on their own.

Coach Coffey paced back and forth with a scowl on his face of disappointment from losing and seeing their behavior.

I hated it too but I had also learned that as a coach you have to pick your battles and trying to make them take a knee at that moment may backfire into something bigger. I respected the patience Browbow had for kids like that.

Browbow held his hand to stop any noise that whispered out toward him.

"Listen up, all eyes on me, tough loss guys, but you know me well enough by now, that I'm not gon' bullshit yall we played a bad game tonight. We can't work as hard as we did to make the playoffs then all of sudden decide to play as bad as we did tonight, not against a good team like that. You can't make mistake, after mistake, after mistake and expect to come out with a victory. Talent ain't enough guys-it's just not enough."

Behind us you could hear cheering and celebration. Browbow paused and let the sound penetrate.

"You hear that sound… all that cheering behind me, remember that sound because we will be back… ain't that right!" he yelled.

"*RIGHT*!" the team responded back in unison.

"Everybody up, put your hands in-up high, on three Warriors… one-two-three *WARRIORS*!"

"Underclassmen, make sure you holla at the seniors, seniors tell the underclassmen something that they need to work on to get us back here next year.

The underclassmen split in every direction so they could shake the hands and slap the shoulder pads of the seniors who had played their last high school game. They had sadness and appreciation in their eyes and faces. A few ninth graders stood off to the side taking in what they hoped one day would be them, a playoff team.

The lights were being shut off which is the signal to get out. We picked up any tape that was left in the grass and as a team we walked back to the visitors' locker room. They packed up their bags and had quiet conversations about the game and we headed out the door back to the buses.

***

On the bus ride home, I always sit alone, second seat behind the bus driver whether we win or lose. Hutch always flanking my right, with his equipment in the chair next to him. Walter usually say in the back but tonight he came and sat down next to Hutch. Walter was silent at first, turned to his teammate and thanked him for having his back all season but especially over this entire year. I swung my legs around and faced them. I chimed in with a thank you of my own.

"I'm proud to have had the pleasure to coach both of yall. You made my job easy and it will be hard two replace players like you."

"Coach, we want to thank you too, youa great coach," Hutch said.

"I try my best, this game has been good to me and I just want to make sure that I give back what was given to me."

"Good luck next year Coach," Walter said.

I swung my legs back and we rode in silence for miles. I sat in peace as I watched two friends ride their last bus ride home together. I was proud of both of them. I meant the sentiments that I confessed from my heart.

Hutch was looking out the window and Walter was leaning back as deep as the bus chair would let him, his eyes closed. It was a two-hour ride home and I am sure they were both thinking of the things I used to think about during rides like this, thoughts of getting out of Youngstown, away from the sounds of gunshots, crime and dead friends.

I reset my shoulder cozily as I could get it between the seat and side of the bus, my head leaning up against the window, my eyes peering out into the night sky. I could feel the dawn of sleepiness overtaking me. I closed my eyes and thought about next year and if I should stay at Southside one more season or pursue my desire to become a head coach.

I was only minutes into my snooze when I could feel my leg being nudged accompanied by the words "Coach-wake up."

I slid back to the edge of the bus seat.

"Yeah what's up Walter?" I asked.

Walter with his elbow bumping Hutch back to consciences.

"Yeah what up," Hutch replied.

"Coach, where do you think we should go to school at?" Walter asked.

"Where you wanna go to school at?" I asked.

"Right now, I'm leaning to OSU, Michigan and Florida State," Hutch said

“What about you Walt?”

“Coach I will go anywhere, as long as it’s away from my father, sometimes I can’t take his doggin’ all the time… I hate it… I hate him to be real wit’ you.”

“Man don’t say that bro, I know he be on your ass man, but maybe he just wants you to shine,” Hutch said.

“It’s easy for you man cause you got all the big schools all over you, I only got small D-2’s and a few HBCU’s and that’s it.”

“Coach J’ already hipped me to all that division shit Walt, he said it don’t matter where you go as long as it’s free and you graduate, so that’s my focus man…I’m getting my paper and getting the fuck outta there, ain’t that right Coach?”

“Right and exact, see Walt we all shad dream of going to the league, making millions of dollars, you know getting out of the hood and all that, but the reality of is this, Ima pull it up on my phone and read it to so that you won’t think I’m making this up.”

I took out my phone, pulled up google and typed in the information.

“Ima read this to yall… *There are 1,093,234 high school football players in the United States, and 6.5% of those high school players (or 71,060) will play in college. The drop off from college to the pros is even more dramatic: only **1.2%** college-level players will get drafted to the NFL.*

So now what, so now think about all the little kids in the youth league, the middle school kids and high school all planning on going to the league, especially the black kids. I was one of them until I got hip to the game. The game of education being on the top of my list and sports being second and eventually not even in my thought process.”

Hutch shrugged his shoulders in agreement with what I had read. Walter’s face looking more confused than before.

They continued to talk.

“Hue, I need some help making my choice of the school to go too. I hate this city and the crib is like a jail when my pops is around,” Walter said.

He pounded his fist on the top of his helmet that sat in his lap.

"My dad been putting pressure on me since I was in little league… he criticize everything I do, I don't work hard enough in the summer, I don't enough in winter conditioning, I need to be doing this, I need to be doing that, but of all the shit he says to me, the shit I hate the most is when he compares me to Yosef. That shit be pissin me off for real.

I try and do everything right so he will get off my ass but the more I do, the more he talks shit about it and acts like he don't see me trying. I work hard Hutch, you see me out there doing my thing… he just don't see it!"

"Coach B got something for you, he hooked you up with some schools and they talking about free rides ain't they? You had a good season and your grades straight right?" Hutch asked.

"Yeah my books straight and I got two full offers, it's just other shit man, stuff I'm going through with my dad and all types of other shit. Isum being locked up, Yosef dead, both missed their last season of high school ball, that's all bad man, that's why I gotta get the fuck outta here."

"What happened with Isum ain't got nothing to do with you, that shit is on him! Hutch said.

"Yeah, but…you right man that shit is on him."

I felt myself softly dozing off and reminiscing on the season and the things I could have done better. Thoughts of 'maybes' took over my mind… maybe I should have taken more of an interest in Isum or being there for Yosef the night he died, or even being better prepared for the playoff game we just lost. Either way all those 'maybes' added up that I was ready for a break and a chance to go home after school and sit in a soft chair before the sun went down.

As the bus moved fast down the highway I folded up my worn out coaching hoodie, and used it for a pillow and looked out the window until I fell asleep.

***

That Monday, the team came to the locker room to turn in their equipment. I looked over at Yosef's locker still decorated but empty from his last game a year ago. I looked at it over-and over again making sure no one touched it other than Marva, but she wasn't here, she just appeared like a hologram in my head, the cheerleaders were gone, the season was over, but still I watched his locker like a madman. Sadness overwhelmed me where I stood as the other coaches collected girdles tossing them into the reconditioning bag that the players missed like a bad free throw shooters.

"See you at weight lifting Coach," a few under classmen said as they went out the door.

"Hey guys the banquet will be on February 21st, in the cafeteria, you will receive a letter in the mail about it and make sure you dress nice, no saggin' pants or you're not getting in!" Big Browbow yelled.

"Aight, Coach, we got you," they replied.

Big Browbow sat down on the bench left of Yosef's locker. He told all the coaches to sit down with him and he thanked us for a good season. We thanked him back.

"I will be in touch over the next few months; right now I have to solidify this recruiting process for the seniors. But when this banquet comes up, I'm serious, we not letting anyone in who has saggin' pants and they behinds showing and I don't care if they are with their parents. 'I'm sick of seeing that prison mentality in this program."

"Coach, where is Hutch going to go school?" asked one of the assistant coaches.

"To be honest, he can go anywhere he wants to go. He has over fifty offers from all the top conferences. His grade point average is good and his A.C.T. score is a twenty-two. The boy did it right, all four years he didn't play around like some of our other boys did and still do, now those same boys are running around trying to get a last minute grade change or turning in missing or late assignments. I wouldn't be mad at one teacher who refused to help any one of them. Kids don't come around often-kids like a Hutch Campbell," Browbow said proudly.

We all stood up, shook hands, many of the assistants immediately heading out the door. A few others lingering behind to help clean up the miscellaneous trash, shoulder pad clips and chewed on mouthpieces that littered the floor.

I went to my locker to retrieve all the clothes that piled up over the season. Three hoodies, a rain suit, baseball caps and nappy winter skullys. I reached deep into the back of the top shelf until my knuckles hit metal. My fingertips fumbled through objects that were familiar to my touch; a whistle, stopwatch, play sheets and a standby bottle of yellow pills just in case I caught an episode at practice, the other bottle was in my car console.

I gathered my belongings, dropping them into my backpack, took a deep breath, and one more look around and walked out the door.

I dreamed I was top of the world watching the world.
Awoke to a room full of smoke, gun at my throat
I dwell in the heart of the hell, but never fell
Po'nine scopin' me the whole time, they close behind

- Inspectah Deck

21

SEASON CLOSED

THE LEAVES HAD fallen was the first thing I wrote in my football journal. I wrote; the excitement that a football season causes was now like the leaves that blew freely across the ground, some still holding beauty but no longer alive or as colorful. The ending of a season brings on a sorrow for all who are involved, and a solace, that only football players can feel and understand. Winter months spent lifting weights and growing together as a team, all in eagerness for the summer that soon comes back around, but like clockwork, it passes again, and each senior class takes on the look of that fallen leaf that blows freely across the ground. Then winter creeps over the dormant grass in waiting of the next group of Warriors ready to dig their cleats into it- The end for now.

The second was my homage to Mr. Jabo Wright. Jabo Wright out lasted all of them, my uncle, and most of the gangsters of his day and for that matter young one's from today.

Jabo Wright got sick when he turned sixty-two and was never the same after that. He was already skinny and being sick gave him the appearance of an old crackhead, but he wasn't anything close to that, he was my uncles friend-his boy-his ace-boon-coon.

His funeral was packed with people his age, some of the faces recognized me and greeted me kindly, and it made me feel good. May you rest in peace Mr. Jabo Wright. He was one of ours.

***

The last few months of winter was spent on college recruiting and placement of the senior football players into someone's university. Browbow did a great job at making sure that the majority of his players would be eligible to receive an athletic or academic scholarship. Nevertheless, each year, no matter how good the season went or how bad, there were always slackers, players who thought football was their world and nothing else mattered to them. No matter how hard the coaches preached grades-grades-grades that message to some, fell-on-deaf ears.

This year the team had seventeen seniors and eleven of the seventeen had earned athletic scholarships. The top one was of course was Hutch, he had garnered First-Team All-State and All-American honors two seasons in a row. He was also the league's Player of the Year and elected to the All-Star Team. Right behind him in accolades was Walter Jameson Jr. who was Second-Team All-State and First-Team All-City as a running back. The others players' awards were scattered from second teams to honorable mentions.

Each year the first Wednesday of February is the National Signing Day for the NCAA. High Schools from across the country hold signing-day ceremonies in their libraries, gyms and auditoriums and Southside High School was no different. This event had become bigger and bigger each year, but this year was the largest because of the press and publicity of having a Hutch Campbell on the team and his performance in the first round of the playoffs despite the loss to Red Castle. Not being foolish, I knew that some of the press was here for Yosef and I anticipated that at least one question about his death would be brought up…and this being his year to get a scholarship, which he would have received, sounded like a good backstory to me. I'm just glad that Browbow had to answer those questions tomorrow and not me.

The day before, I was walking to the men's room when the corner of my eye saw Walter Jr sitting in the auditorium. It was eighth period, his study hall. I walked over to him. He was looking over the letters of scholarships he had been offered. One to a Mid-Major Division-1 and the other, to a Historically Black College, Charles Young University a Division-2 in the South. I knew he wanted to attend CYU but the gambler in me bet that his father would disapprove and I bet he knew it too.

I sat down next to him. I wondered if Hutch or any other of his teammates had to deal with what he was about to deal with. Probably not I thought.

I decided to take a proactive approach. I asked Walter to convince his father to stop by my classroom after school so I could buffer the conversation about tomorrows signing day.

Walter pulled out his cell phone to text his father. His fingers rapidly striking the tiny keys typing in his request for an impromptu parent-teacher meeting. After a few minutes, he lifted up his head showing the universal cell phone posture of receiving an answer from the person on the other end.

"What he say?" I asked.

"At first he asked me what you wanted…but then said okay and that he would stop up here as soon as he cleared the building."

Walter slammed his shoulders back into the wooden backstop of the auditorium seat. We sat for a few minutes more then headed to my classroom to wait for his father.

***

A hard knock on my door startled me. I opened it and without a false step, Jameson militarily walks into my room. I could see Walt Jr's posture become stiff and ridged. He readied himself because he knew how this would turn out. His father was a hard man to talk too, nevertheless convince of anything that he felt strongly about but we had to at least try.

"What up Coach, thanks for the invite. Jameson said looking around as if he landed on Mars.

"Grab a seat and let's talk about tomorrow," I said asked as he sat next to his son in my classroom desks.

"Pops, I asked your son to get you up here, because I know that he still hasn't declared where he will be attending college in the fall and I wasn't sure either, but I didn't want him to wait until tomorrow when the mic is in his face to figure this out."

"Walter, tell us where your mind is at with all this."

"I'm jus' trying to decide what to do," he said shyly.

"That's easy son, we going D-1 right," his father answered with slight doubt in his voice.

"I don't know, I sorta wanna to go to the black school, they really want me and they have what I wnt to study," Walter said with a little hesitation, afraid to look directly at his father.

"Hah-boy, what you scared of, go play with the big boys, those southern boys don't play no type real ball down there, it's cool-but it's small time, it's D2 ball, ain't that right Coach!"

"Dad, I'm going to Charles Young. I'm the one who has to be there for four years not you or ma, but me, that's how Coach Browbow told me how to look at it."

"Well I don't give a fuck about what Browbow said. I ain't signing the contract or letter of intent and you mother ain't either and that's the end of that. You talking stupid son. Who picks D2 over D1? Only a chump that's who, and I didn't raise no damn chumps, so in the morning-when I head to that auditorium for the signing day ceremony, you gonna sign the right paper, or go join the Navy or some shit, but you not gonna be chillin' round here in this punk-ass city, or down at some poo-butt-bum-black-college. Now, if you got some money stashed away that me or your mother don't know about, then you free to spend it wherever you like."

"It's' my life and should be my choice," Walter said.

"You hear this shit Ant?" His father asked me. "This boy is…."

You could now clearly see that Jameson was making himself stay calm to deal with his son with a level head and not continue to speak from emotion and anger.

"Son, my career didn't go as I planned. Your grandfather really didn't give a shit about me or any of your uncles playing sports. He was old-school, he was all about going to work and taking care of home, the same shit I do 'round here for you and your mother and little sister, and all of that is cool. I told myself if I have a son I was gonna be involved in his sports life. I want the best for you that's why I push you so hard, I didn't get that push. I know what's best for you…" Walter Jr. interrupts. "But Coach Browbow said that…"

Angered by the few words he let his son get out of his mouth. Jameson jumps up from the desk and starts yelling and pointing his finger in his sons face. "See, you too damn busy listening to everybody else other than me. I coulda went to the league, but I fucked up on my grades and didn't have anyone pushing me. Then my coaches sucked too, they really didn't look out for me, just like Browbow only really lookin' out for Hutch. So I ain't lettin' you make no dumb-ass choice like turning down a bigger school for a small one. It's all about exposure son, the NFL gonna look big before they look small.

Don't get me wrong son, CYU was a nice campus, we had a great time on your visit but I know you can play D-1."

Walter had a look of defeat on his face. He is in a place of can't-win or better yet don't-know-how-to-win and why-even-try-to-win. I could tell he had so much he wanted to tell his father but he held it in and took his verbal lashing.

"Jameson listen… Walt and I talked about this several times and I know I'm not his parent but at least hear him out man," I said.

Jameson looked up at me and said nothing. His facial expression said it all and that was to mind my business but he was in my room standing on my invitation, which he could has easily turned down. He didn't and I now I'm wondering why.

His father left as he came with Walter Jr. in tow. You could hear part two of the same conversation-taking place as they walked down the hallway. I felt weak because I just stood there and never spoke my peace on it. I went home that night feeling as if I let Walter Jr down.

That evening I called him.

"You good?" I asked him.

"Yeah Coach. I'm good...I guess."

He sounded confused and dejected. I felt sorry for him and wanted to help him anyway that I could. "

"What happened when you got home did you and your father talk some more?"

"He did most of the talking, then, my mom got involved."

"What happened?" I asked him.

"My father told my mother that she needed talk to *her* son, because I pissed him off and that he was tryin' to guide me but that I got my mind someplace else."

"What did she say when he said that?"

"She defended me, she said that I am old enough to make this decision on my own, and that I have to live with it. She said what difference does it make where I go to school, as long as the school is free and as long as I liked it, then I should be able to make my own choice."

Walter paused mid-stream. I guess trying to recollect the entire conversation.

He continued.

"Then my father said. I hear you, but the problem is that I need to challenge myself with better players, better competition. He said I already played for sorry ass Coach Browbow and his coaching staff. I played on the junior varsity squad for three years and if Yosef wouldna died- then I woulda just been a bench warmer my senior season. He said, that I got talent and he not gonna let me waste it or the chance that he didn't have… then my mother said…how many times are you gonna keep saying that? The chance that you didn't have, the coach this and the coach that, she said that she wished that I woulda quit football a long time ago. She said that he did a good job raising me, and that people respect him and appreciate what he does in the community, but that I am his only son and that he should treat me better than his father treated him and his brothers. She then started mumbling about hating damn football. She always told me it was bad back when my father played in high school, but now he was living through me. She told me to be my own man and not my dad.

Bottom line Coach is, he ain't gonna sign my letter of intent unless it's D-1. Last thing my mother said was that he was gonna ruin my life. He walked out after that."

I thought I could safely say that he probably was used to hearing them argue especially when it had to do with football. I suggested that he take advantage of the chance given to get out of the house and clear his head.

"Okay Coach, I do need to get some air."

I could hear him rustling in the background.

"I don't have any place to go Coach, but I will find me a destination."

"Just go someplace where you can sit and think, and call me if you need to talk some more, okay?"

"Okay."

***

I was tired. My body moved slowly but my mind was running off the fumes of emotion and impulse. The night air was brisk and after about fifteen minutes of sitting. I walked outside looking up and down the street in hopes I could catch a mid-evening breeze. I thought about the L, wondering if he went there, but why would anyone in his or her right mind go there? I started to worry about Walter and the possible bad advice I gave him telling him to leave his home. I overstepped my bounds with irresponsible quick words. I put on my jacket and started walking down the street and looking over my shoulder just in case a jumper was lurking in the shadows. I put myself in his shoes and that navigated me toward the stadium. I walked down Oakhill Avenue and made a b-line down to the top of Delason past the cleaner part of the L. I could smell the rust and ash from the hollow Republic Steel Mill that hovered in the distance of the stadium. I unlocked the gate, looked around in the obvious places but there was no sight of him. The air was starting to bother me-the coldness of it. I yelled out his name. Through the wind, I could faintly hear him responding to my cries.

"Where are you?" I yelled out.

I could see a single silhouette sitting alone through an illuminated backlit corner street light, standing over the top railing of the bleachers right above the spot where Yosef was found-covered in chocolate milk.

"Up here Coach," he said.

"Come up Coach," he commanded.

"Your parents know your here?" I asked.

"Naw, they don't know."

"How long were you planning on staying up here in the bleachers, its cold out here."

"I don't know Coach, you said find a place to think, so this is where I came, but what made you look here?" he said.

"Of course I was going to show up here, common sense I guess-and you need me right about now, so no matter the time, no matter the situation, if you or any players need me or any of the coaches we will be here for you. Listen Walter, I gave you some bad advice, telling you to leave tonight. I was wrong. It's not my place to tell you to leave your house this time of night."

"But Coach, I'm glad you did, cause I need to get away from my crib."

Walter never called on any of the coaches for help, because he knew his father would not approve as if they were replacing him as his father, so a lot of the times Walter would either talk to Isum, Yosef or Hutch. But this time, was he was pressed and desperate. I had found out about the gun they shared and their reasons for carrying it. I asked around and searched for more answer on Yosef's death, whether he committed suicide or died by accident. I spoke with his grandparents and tried to help ease their grief, all of these things leading to paths of nothingness and heartache. All the stories, scenarios, maybes, probably, possibly-all made the ingredients for a devils chili recipe.

Walter stood up and reached in his back pocket to pull out the scholarship letters he had with him. He looked at them and shuffled them around like playing cards. He looked at me and asked, "You ever have to make a choice like this?" I took the letters and smiled in remembrance of the time when I held those same pieces of mail that represented a small type of freedom in my hand.

"Years ago, I did, my uncle helped me out with it, it worked out for me."

"I believe it, but my father ain't your uncle."

Walter looked across the L and placed his hands on his knees. You could tell he had a lot on his young mind.

"I mean right now Coach, tomorrow is a big day for me, for all of us…Yosef…I wish Yosef could be here tomorrow," he starts to cry. "And my dad acts like he don't care about that part. He never liked Yosef. He said you suck as a coach and Yosef was-overrated as a player, and that Coach B catered to him. Coach I ain't signing with the D-1 school. My father is all hyped up about it and he don't care if they was selling crack to the players, it's D-1 and that is all he cares about…

it makes him look good, and to keep it real, I don't even care if I never go to school, I just gotta get away from him."

We sat looking across the dark field not saying anything but surely thinking of what to say next. I broke the silence first and in a random cadence, I told Walter that I love my father. Walter looking at me asked. "How do you love some dude who you don't even know just 'cause he your father?" That question proving to me that Walter remembered me saying words about my Dad.

"Good question, but I have a better answer. Honor thy mother and father, that's how. What my father decided to not do is on him-not me, same for my mother, but I still have to honor them, so I do love them and honor them each day by trying my best to follow God's laws and commandments… your dad loves you Walter, I promise he does."

"Yeah, I know he does… me and Isum talked the other night on the phone, he said you been in his ear about a lot of stuff, that's it's helping him a lot. That's cool Coach, seems like we all need your help," Walter said.

"I needed help back in my days and even today, I try hard to be a good example for ya'll, it ain't always easy but I have to do it."

"It's still hard for me Coach to understand how you can care or love a dude you don't even talk too?" Walter asked again.

"Love for a parent can't leave your body, you just hide it away, cover it up for a while, say things like-my dad ain't this-he ain't that, all just to hide that you miss him or you wish he was around. Your father ain't perfect, but he is around and cares for you, believe that. Whatever it is that you need to express to your dad, then do it, he is gon-say-what-he-gon-say and then just go from there."

"I know Coach, but I messed up with all of this," Walter said looking down between his legs.

"You and your dad having a fight, you not going home, him being on your case all the time about football, all that is part of growing up in Youngstown because people around here love football, sometimes too much, especially fathers. Everything else that happens to us is part of our curses and things we have to go through. Tomorrow, stand strong, be respectful, and pick a school and deal with your father afterwards and I will have Coach Browbow talk with him too. But for now it's time go home and pray about it, try to get some sleep."

From a distance, you could see headlights coming down Erie Street. It was Walter's mother. I texted her and told our whereabouts and apologized for the misstep with her son. She got out of the car and as she approached the bleachers, you could see she her face was grimaced and her stride upset.

"Evening Coach, she said without looking my way. "Walter, me and your father had a big fight about this college thing. I'm at home trying to defend you and you out here running the streets, where were you running too son? You can't avoid your father. I drove around to a few places looking for you, until Coach Jones texted me but I should have come here first anyway," she said.

Your father is wrong, he thinks he can live through you, he thinks that he is right, he loves you, but has trouble expressing it to you and even to me sometimes. Tomorrow, you can pick the school that you want to pick, be true to yourself and be happy about the decision- okay… and don't worry I will handle your father like I always do."

She hugged him and turns to me. "Coach, thank you for caring about my son, he needs people like you in his life."

That made me smile as they walked away. I stood alone for a few more minutes more, listening to the ghostly sounds of a crowd that once cheered for me. I headed home. When I opened the door, Adrienne was sitting in my living room. Her beautiful face lowered due to my late arrival from helping another kid.

As I walked in the door, I said to myself, *good luck to me*.

Or maybe I'm blowing this shit out of proportion
But this shit do happen to niggas very often
So fuck it, a nigga gotta do what he meant to
My crew got my back, fuck the world is my mental

- Mobb Deep

22

PUDDLE OF MUD

Adrienne was quiet most of the evening. It takes her a while to quell her temper and with all this going on, I didn't really care about her being mad at me. My attention was on Walter, Isum and Yosef. Yet, in the back part of my mind smaller thoughts led to present-time, of Yosef today. I envisioned him sitting on the stage next to Hutch with his grandparents behind him proud and proper, Yosef grabbing his pen, assembling his papers, and signing his name to attend The Ohio State University, nobody knew he wanted to go there but me. His future was bright and then it dimmed, like a candle in the wind. He would have made good, graduated from college and had a chance to be great. I believe that he would have.

Maybe, his parents would read about him in the paper or see him on the news and maybe, just maybe, regret giving him up. Maybe, his mother would feel the guilt of what she put him through now seeing him make a way for himself. His grandparents, they should be celebrated, for taking him from her and providing him a life of love and care.

Maybe, when they read about him, they would come clean, or get clean and come and parent him, so I wouldna had to do it...maybe.

Yosef is dead-remember? I had to snap my thoughts back to reality. Yosef is dead. His face keeps calling me; the image of him down is a burden on me. I wish I never met him; this is so heavy on me. Why did he have to find me that day? I wish I hated him, then I wouldn't love him so. Adrienne said that I need help, that I should talk to someone, that I should flush those pills down the toilet. I can't because I am addicted. I can't because I am afraid of what may happen as I watch them swirl down the bowl. I am addicted to dreams of a little boy that is dead, now I cannot kick the habit of thinking and dreaming of him.

The television is watching me. Adrienne is talking but I can't hear her. I'm in a trance of fear and anxiety. I got up from the couch and walked to the back room that I closed off from the world years ago. I unlocked the door, closing it behind me. I'm in Yosef's room, my room, my uncles' room, our room. I stood in the middle of the floor stretching out my arms like Christ, hoping for that nail to pin my soul to God. My breathing got deep but under control. I could feel a calmness overtake me like a warm blanket in winter. I closed my eyes as tight as I could. I see myself as a child, then as a teenager, and now, as a grown man. All the mistakes that I had ever made I atoned for them now.

I returned to the couch as not to cause her to worry or come looking for me. I tried my best to focus on what was on the tube but my eyes dragged up to the mantelpiece and my favorite things from past and present.

A knock on the door dropped my eyes in wonder of who was standing in the backlit shadows of my uncovered porch light. I pulled back the white sheer curtains that Adrienne got for me to add class to my door. It was Stretch. I smiled. He opened his arms up as if to say "what-up" without speaking any words.

I opened the door and invited him in. He stepped gently through the threshold. His eyes brightened from the view of Adrienne sitting lovely on my couch.

"Adrienne this is my one of my childhood friends, Stretch."

"Nice meeting you Stretch," she greeted.

"Same here," Stretch said.

Adrienne was conditioned from years of visitors who tap on my door at godless hours that a meeting in private was about to happen and since this was the first time she had ever seen or heard of a character in my life named "Stretch" she automatically knew that Stretch and I were heading down into the basement.

Stretch walked behind me and I could tell he was having a blast from the past. He had been in this house several times when we were kids running in the front door and out the back. I could tell being back in here made him feel good inside, the happiness showed in the curiosity of his head turning in all directions.

We made our way down to the basement, a place Stretch or any of my childhood friends had never been. This was the forbidden part of the house from any civilian except for Jabo Wright. Stretch's eyes widened as the darkness grew larger and larger. My uncle was long gone but I paid homage to him by keeping it as dark as I could down here. Adrienne thought that was strange but for me it was an honor.

I opened the same door to the room under the kitchen-my man cave. It was still under construction but not enough that I couldn't bring company down here or sit alone to read a book or watch TV in comfort.

"This some nice shit Ant," Stretch said.

"Thanks, been working on it for years."

"Yeah-man, aaahhh, I bet you tripped out when you saw me at the door huh."

"Light-weight," I said.

"You got something to drink?" he asked me.

"No-doubt-what you want?"

"Some Henn if you got any."

I had an unopened bottle of Hennessy that I displayed as a showpiece only. I didn't drink and Adrienne only drank wine. I never had company, so I never thought a request would be put in for it to be opened. I ran upstairs, grabbed two shot glasses and the Hennessey. I poured us both up to the rim. I balanced the drinks as I headed back down to the basement. Stretch was up admiring my old awards and pictures hanging on the walls.

"Your uncle was a good dude Antietam-a real good dude."

"Yeah he was…he saved my life."

"Peace be upon him," he said.

I didn't respond back to him. I found myself engulfed in the words "Peace be upon him."

I handed him his drink.

"Toast to Mr. Smith," Stretch said hosting up his glass.

"Yeah-toast to my uncle Kay-Kee Smith."

We sat down. He on the couch and me on the plush theater seat cattycorner to the 58 inch Television.

"So what's up Stretch?"

"That day you left the crib, me and Deaf-P could tell that you fucked up over what happened to your player."

"I'd be lying to say I ain't fucked up, that's for sure."

"Cops aint' saying shit are they?"

"Cold case," I answered.

"Shit every niggah that's dead in Youngstown is a cold case," he said.

"Basically."

"Ant, you know I been out here in the streets for a while now. Shit is getting old man, I gotta get myself a real job and a crib, can't keep living of schemes and scams man. Gotta get a house like you and a woman that will take care of me. Man- what I'm asking is can you get me a job at the school?

I was on the internet and I saw that Southside was looking for an assistant maintenance man. You know I'm good with fixing shit and whatnot…can you plug me in?"

"Ima be straight with you Stretch. If you got any felonies then they ain't even gonna look at your resume…but if you clean, then hell yeah I will help you any way I can."

"Ant I'm clean man, ain't never been to jail or in court, at least for no serious shit anyway. Maybe God been looking out for me all these years keeping me out the bing and now I run into you."

"Man-God been looking out for both of us…get me a resume ASAP and I will do the rest. Oh yeah, you got a suit?"

"Nah-but I will today."

"Cool."

"Aight, I aint gone take no more time from you and your lady," he said.

"Stretch, you know this house is your house brother, come by anytime you need or want too."

We walked back upstairs to the front door. He greeted Adrienne once again with a "nice meeting you."

"You too, Anthony I'm leaving, I have to stop by my mother's house before I go home," she said.

I walked Adrienne to her car. I could see Stretch through the picture window standing in front of the mantle in the living room.

The first thing he picked up was Yosef's helmet. I could instantly feel boiling pressure in my bones asking myself why he is touching it. He didn't know the significance that a plastic helmet could hold inside…the power of a genies lamp rubbed for three wishes…the prayers for a dead boy…the only thing left of him to hold on too. He couldn't see Yosef's face behind the red facemask smiling back at me after a big run.

Stretch turned the helmet back and forth and with each tumult, I flinched in fear of him dropping it and watching it shatter like a glass vase. I ran back in the house.

I walked over to him and held out my hands. He placed the helmet in my palms, the warmth that I was feeling quickly went away and my mind was back to normal.

Sensing his error.

"My fault Ant," he said.

"You didn't know…it's the only thing I have left of him."

Stretch reached out his hand and we shook.

Before he walked onto the porch, he turned to me and said.

"Man, since when did you start drinking?"

"I still don't, that was ginger ale in my glass."

We shared a laugh and he departed from my sight.

***

I had placed Yosef's helmet in the far right corner next to my uncles letter S. I wanted it up there because it was special to me and no longer deserved to be on anyone else's head other than his. I had never really looked at it in detail until Stretch unknowingly violated this space.

I picked it up. I held it at arm's length, thought again about his face behind the mask smiling at me. His helmet was beautiful to me, a part of my life that meant a lot to me. I turned it over looking inside at all the intricate pads covered with particles of dirt and grass clippings from the last game he played. *A game worn helmet,* I thought to myself.

Caked up mud was up under the pads and around the inner earholes. I got a wet cloth to clean off certain parts because that is what Yosef would have done-he liked to look good. I wiped hard to remove the dirt that had set for over a year. In my efforts, I uncovered three initials that read WJJ-11.

***

Every piece of equipment that we pass out is logged in, name, size and model number. We initialize each helmet too, in case a player tries to switch it off for a better facemask or more popular style. We always made sure our best players got the best equipment because they would be the ones playing on Friday nights. *Did I have the wrong helmet?* I thought. How?-if I did. Yosef's grandfather gave me his practice bag with the helmet inside. I brought it directly here. I didn't stop anywhere or talk with anyone other than Adrienne and she wouldn't touch it. This login *WJJ-11* is not making sense to me. I began beating my common sense for a logical answer but I came up with nothing.

I took the helmet to my room and sat it on the dresser. I pulled off my shirt from the day and fell back onto my bed as if it were a pool of water. It bounced me back up only for me to softly land again. I kicked off one of my shoes and let out a loud sigh.

I went to sleep with a heavy mind.

***

I woke up early and drove directly to the locker room. I keyed into Coach Browbow's office to retrieve the 2005 equipment login sheet. I started at the top and fingered my way down every name making sure that every helmet matched up with what was passed-out, and what was turned-in. I went back a year in the logbook. I had the so-called Yosef helmet for a year.

"No record of its login after his death." I said aloud.

I wasn't looking for Yosef's name but I was looking for WJJ-11. I made my way to the J's.

Jackson- ZJ-67 (Zion Jackson- Helmet #67)

Janks KJ-43 (Karlton Janks- Helmet # 43)

Jameson-WJJ-11 (Walter Jameson Jr- Helmet #11, issued on July 15)

I wasn't sure what to think. Kids steal helmets and jerseys all the time, but Yosef's helmet was found at his side the night of the accident. Where is it?

I sank backwards in time. All the stories and conversations rewinding like a movie going backwards on a screen. Isum said that he and Walt walked away and left Yosef alone that night. Marva said that she was with Yosef at the top of the bleachers but left with her parents, a story which they corroborate. Raquel gave me no real information. MK loosened up a few screws. Mr. Hall seemed to insinuate that Mrs. Browbow hated Yosef that she may have killed him. Officer Jameson claims it was an accident or suicide-without saying suicide. Haso and P helped a little but not enough. I shoulda took that five-thousand for the trouble I have been through…naw I don't mean that at all. Detective Madison closed his case and moved on, but something don't sit well with me, really never has since that terrible day. His grandparents trusted me back then and I need to find out what is going on, even if it is nothing but my imagination.

Outsiders were stuck, by enemies who put fear
And blasted on the spot before the pigs were there
You know hoods, robbers, snipers new in sight
Fuck blue and white
They escape before them flash the fucking lights
Gunshots, shatter first-floor window panes
Shells hit the ground and blood stained the dice game.

- GZA JUSTICE

23

FEBRUARY 3rd

IN THE SMALL auditorium, the Athletic Director Daryl Forrest, Secretary Jorge and Coach Browbow dressed two large tables on the stage with a blue tablecloth and a large red table sash with the Southside Warrior emblem embroidered on the front. A dark wooden podium with a microphone was between the tables. Twelve chairs with twelve nametags aligned at the edge of the table. Local news stations where setting up in their assigned places to get the best shots and coverage of the big event. Streamers and balloons hung in unison to create a party like scene.

I was dressed in a red tie and black dress pants to look appropriate for the signing day ceremony. I had decide to bring Yosef's helmet with me to the signing. I sat it on the table next to his name tag because even though he was dead, he still deserved his place at the table.

The underclassmen football players gathered outside the mid-sized auditorium and I directed them to a special section of seating directly below the stage. The room was rapidly filling up with teachers, youth football coaches, friends and community members who supported and loved the program.

The parents of each signee stood behind their sons chairs to wait for start and the official signings of the scholarship letters packaged strategically by each universities compliance officer. Coach Browbow stepped up to the Microphone prepared his notes for the introduction of his scholarship recipients.

I stood in the back of the stage with the boys making sure their ties and shirts were in order before they took their seats. Walter Jr. stood off to the side peering out of the split in the backstage curtain. I walked over to him to inquire about the helmet. He looked down at it and then up at me, but only for a second. His eyes wondered away quickly. I could tell that seeing that asking him about the helmet triggered something inside of him.

"I have your helmet Walt." I said to him with a set-up in mind. I was fishing no doubt, not sure what I was looking to catch, maybe nothing at all but I had run out of answers and was ready to accept defeat.

"That's your helmet sitting up there next to Yosef's name ain't it? I asked.

"I turned my helmet in Coach after that last game we played." He answered back.

I walked back up on the stage and grabbed the helmet and took over to Walter. I turned it over and found a crease of light that shined beyond the black curtain, just enough for him to see his initials inscribe inside. As he looked squinting, I studied his face for any expression that could set off alarms in my mind. He looked at the initials.

"Coach, this is my helmet from last season. I turned it in," he said.

"I'm not saying that you didn't Walter, but I got your helmet from Mr. and Mrs. Nassy, Yosef's grandparents. How did they end up with it if you turned it in?" I asked him.

"I don't know Coach, maybe…"

"Maybe what Walt, maybe you forgot to turn it in," me giving him an out.

"Yeah I think I did forget." Walter taking the avenue that I provided.

"Or maybe you have Yosef's helmet." I asked him.

"Huh, why would I have his helmet Coach?" He asked me.

"Well, I been thinking about that same question Walter and it didn't come to me until this morning. The whole story came to me, a story that I hope I am wrong about."

"Story-ain't no story Coach."

Walter began to fidget and in the background, you could hear Big Browbow start the opening of the program. I ran the helmet back to the table and ducked out of site.

"Good afternoon, I would first like to say that it is great to see all the people who came out today, some of you are skipping work to be here. I hope you will still have a job when you leave here," the crowd laughed. "Because you'll know this will be on the news, but seriously, I am proud to be here today to celebrate this fine group of student-athletes. They have earned the right to be up here on this stage. They have worked hard not only on the playing field, but more importantly in the classroom."

"That's right!" someone shouted from the floor.

"I wanted to also thank the parents and grandparents, who love and support these young men, let's give them a round of applause before we continue…so let's get to the real reason why we are here today, the announcement and signing of the football scholarships.

The players' name that I call will walk out with their parents. They will take their place on the stage and I will say a little bit about them and they will be given a chance to say a few words, then the student-athlete will sign his name first and the parents will follow with their signatures last. Please hold all applause until all the student-athletes have all been called and given a chance to say a few words."

Excitement was in the room. The media readied their feet and camera angles and lenses. Reporters reached out with big microphones and sound booms.

Browbow called out the players and their escorts. They sat down as instructed and now the individual speeches and signings would commence. Yosef's spot was empty.

"The first young man is our Quarterback and Captain. This young man started for four years, he is one of the best players I have seen in this area in a long time. He will go down as one of the schools' greatest players if not the greatest in my opinion. He has over fifty scholarship offers from schools all over the country and he will be hard to replace not only as a player but as a leader around the school. Hutch Campbell will be the first one to announce his college destination and sign his papers. He is joined by his parents Mr. and Mrs. Campbell."

Hutch was dressed in a white shirt, a royal blue bowtie and red dress pants. His hair, was skillfully tapered on the sides, with one diamond earring in his left ear. He walked to his chair, stood erect, neatened himself, sat down and began his comments.

"Coach B, I want to thank you for being a great coach and leader to all of us, but especially to me. You gave me the chance to be the starting quarterback as a freshman when you could have put anyone in there to do it but you trusted me. I hope that I didn't disappoint you because I tried my best each year, me and the team. Coach Jones, I'm glad you were my positon coach and taught me how to be a QB-thank you. I will forever be grateful to you for talking to me on and off the field when I needed to talk, it meant a lot and always will… thank you Coach. To my teammates and coaches, I love all yall and I wish yall the best next year at college and here next season at Southside High. To my parents, I want to say I love yall and I hope I made yall proud."

He picks up the pen and signs his name along with his parents.

Browbow steps back up to the microphone to announce the second player.

"Next up is Thomas Harris. This young man is special to me. He was the player that made sacrifices to play anywhere we needed him to play; he played fullback, guard, and punter.

Being not only able but also willing, is what makes him so versatile and valuable to our team. But where he made a name for himself was on defense and he will play outside linebacker on the next level."

Clearing his throat, Tommy begins. "Uuummm-yeah-you know-uumm, thanks Coach for the season, and thanks to Mrs. Nicole and the cheerleaders for all the delicious cookies and treats yall hooked us up with all season." The crowd laughed. "And I want to thank my moms and pops for comin' to all my games since I was little. Ima miss yall dudes for-real, all the 2-a-day practices and Coach Williams always making us run sprints because we gave up points on defense, that part I ain't gonna miss." He gave a big smile and sat down.

Next, T-Lee Chism, the co-captain. He stood up and stepped behind his chair in the middle of his mother and four sisters.

"Hey, I want to thank allllll-yall. We balled out this year, thanks to my mother and father and all my sisters, Southside Warriors for life. Hey-man, we lost that play-off game but it was still fun to be in the play-offs, next year we will be back and we gonna win, underclassman make sure yall get ready for next year, get in that weight room." He sat down with his arms raised in the air as he always did.

The next six players went one by one; the tenth player announced was Walter Jr. with his father standing arrogantly close to the back of his chair in his police uniform. Walter never spoke another word to me or even looked at me the rest of time we were backstage. I didn't press him anymore about the helmet. I decided to wait until this was over and go in for my final strike.

"And now, our next young man, who did a great job for us this season, filling in some big shoes but came into his own. When we needed him to step up he did, and I am proud of him. He rushed for one-thousand and twenty-seven yards and fourteen touchdowns… Walter Jameson Jr. Not only is Junior a great player, but his father Officer Walter Jameson Sr. was a great player here back in the late 80's, along with our own Coach Antietam Jones."

I peeked my head around the curtain, and smiles and loud applause greeted me. I faded back into the darkness not wanting to draw anymore-unwanted attention to Walter's moment on stage.

Walter Jr. stood up like T-lee but then quickly sat down then suddenly skated his chair backwards and rose back up slowly in the manner that a politician would do at a town hall meeting. He straightened out his tie, took a deep breath and began the speech I assumed he spent all night rehearsing in his head probably barely sleeping, because his eyes looked red and fatigued.

"Aaaahh… first I want to thank Coach Browbow and all the coaches for giving me a chance this year to play. I want to thank my teammates and tell yall it was great playing with yall all these years."

He hesitates.

"I wanted to take a minute to talk about our teammate and my friend Yosef Nassy." Choking up-his voice begins to quiver.

"He was a great player and he should be, or would be, sitting up here in this spot instead of me, but he's not."

His father's eyes squinting in misunderstanding of his son's words. He moved forward further pressing the nose of the chair into the back of his son's legs, serving as a warning to stop with his words. His father placed his hand on the back of his son's shoulder blade.

Walter subtly moved forward loosening the grip of his father's hand. Walter tried to step farther away out of his reach, but not to cause an obvious scene. He continued.

"Yosef was better than me, a better player, a better student and my father thinks that too…he always told me that, whenever he had the chance to say it to me he did."

His father faded back almost out of sight with a startled look on his face.

"I earned this scholarship didn't I Coach? He looked back at me for acknowledgement. I stepped out of my shadow of the stage curtain and nodded yes.

"I earned it, because of my play on the field and because of my school work, but my father was right, I still ain't better than Yosef. He was the real deal out there and a good friend too… my dad always had something negative to say about him and the coaches, and how they showed favoritism, but he was wrong."

I was now shook because of the energy that was in the air from Walter Jr.'s words. I immediately felt in my heart that I was to blame for what he was saying but felt proud at the same time for Walter being as bold as a lion. Suddenly Officer Jameson reappears back under the light of the auditorium. He turns his back to the crowd and asks his son why he is doing this.

Big Browbow shouts from the podium "let the boy finish."

Walter's mother grabs her husband's arm and pulls him back into the shadow of the stage, down to bottom of the short stairwell, far behind the black curtain.

"Let him speak," she said quietly in his ear.

"He is making a fool of himself and of me, like I'm some kind of monster of a father to him," as he yanks away from her but does not leave the stairwell.

Walter Jr. looked over the crowd, he looked down the table to his left at Hutch who gave him a smile of confidence to keep going, he looked at Raquel at the bottom of the stage writing it all down, she winked her eye at him. He looked out of the rectangular windows that faced the L, then his lungs ascended high pushing the knot of his tie to the bottom of his chin.

"Coach B, Coach Jones, that night Yosef died in the rain was my fault…Coach, it wasn't no accident… I killed him," he said confidently.

Many people in the crowd rose to their feat in a gasp. The news reporters' rushed forward with their cameras zooming in on Walter's face and sticking out their hand held microphones as far as their arms would allow.

"I hated Yosef, but I loved him too…you know what I mean Coach Jones…how you could hate someone but love them at the same time. I was jealous of Yosef. I can admit that now. I didn't mean to kill him… that night, after the game, I saw him and Marva talking in the bleachers. I could tell it was a heated conversation they was having…I knew what she was telling him…I have known for a while…me and Isum started to walk home and that is when it started.

Yeah, Isum is in jail because of me too. No one was supposed to get hurt that night. I just wanted Yosef to get jumped by them five boys but it didn't work out that way because Yosef stayed in the bleachers. Then I ran and Isum got jumped by them instead and I left Isum like a coward, so he had no choice but to pull that gun and it went all bad from there… I couldn't stop what was already in motion, cause then Isum woulda known that it was a set up.

The once happy room exploded in chaos. Walter's father emerges from the shadow and grabs his son pulling him close to him.

Whispers and mummers quickly filled the room that was clearly in shock. Someone yelled- "this niggah killed Yosef." People began to move all over the place like a kicked beehive, talking and yelling in the disbelief of what just took place. I ran up to the stage to create a blockade with Coach Browbow to prevent people from bum-rushing Walter and his family. Browbow held out his hands like two brown stop signs to slow down the reporters jockeying for a spot to make a live report.

Browbow began yelling as loud as he could for the players to get to the locker room. Hutch and the other boys jumped down and started ushering their teammates away into the hall. Many of the players did as directed, but many of them tried to attack Walter, that is when I came out of my usually calm bag and prepared myself to fight anyone attempting to lift a foot to come on the stage.

Van Staples yelled back at me. “You ain’t gon’ touch me.” I looked at him and thought *if he comes up here, I may have to hit this boy.* Van Staples was one of the few problem kids that played on the team and used this opportunity to challenge me.

“Van, if I was you, I would listen and do as you were told to do, go in the other direction and count this as your last day on this team too!” I said angrily. *We shoulda’ got rid of him a long time ago*, I thought.

“Fuck dis’ team, I don’t giva fuck,” Van hollered. Van looked up at Walter Jr. and said. “You gon’ get your ass dusted on the street, yo pops can’t protect you all the time-niggah.”

Walter’s father jumps at Van and says in an enraged voice, “little boy you threaten my son again, I’ma forget I’m an adult and a policeman and stomp your little ass down.”

Van puffs up his chest acting as if he is up to the challenge. He waves his hand at Officer Jameson and runs out of the auditorium blending in with the madness of the crowd. Chaos has taken over the once honorable ceremony and has now turned in to a scene comparable to a parking lot fight at a club.

Coach Browbow continued to instruct the team to head to the locker room and for all the coaches to escort them there immediately. The news gathered at the foot of the stage surrounding Coach Browbow.

“So this was a confession to a murder Coach?” a reporter rudely asked bumping his way through the crowd of people.

“No, he said boldly. “This is a young man who told his truth and obviously about things we all had no idea about… thank you,” as he hurried out of the backstage exit door.

The Assistant Principal took Walter and his parents and escorted them to Browbow’s office to wait for him and the Police to arrive. I followed behind them. Once there Browbow locked the door. Me and another teacher secured the office area, making sure no reporters got through.

The door opened and Coach Browbow directed me to come into the room. I sat down in a far corner leaning forward-facing Walter and his parents.

The room sat silent until a knock on the door broke the calm. It was the Secretary Jorge. She peeked through the door swiveling her head to find Browbow's location.

"Principal Browbow, there is a student out here who says she needs to speak to you and that's it's an emergency."

Browbow annoyed by her interruption in the midst of a crisis that will possibly make the national news within hours or even minutes.

"Ms. Jorge, please tell whoever it is that this is a bad time."

"I told her that but she refuses to leave until she talks to you, but you may want to talk to her," she said with worry for her boss in her eyes.

"What is it about?" he asked.

Ms. Jorge walks up to Browbow, whispers in his ear a message that changed his face and body language instantly.

"Tell her to give me a few minutes."

"Okay."

***

Detective Madison, who was appointed to the case a year and a half ago, arrived first. He instructed Walter Jr. to sit down in-between his parents, and that his father was not a cop right now but his Dad.

Madison used to be one-time, but moved up to detective shirt and tie. He was one of the good ones. I mean good in terms of doing his job the right way. He was from Farrell PA. He caught a transfer to YPD after his rookie year. I met him on a late night creep that I was on and got jammed up speeding 45 in a 25, not sure why I was speeding home, I was single at the time and didn't have rush home to anyone. He pulled me over wrote me a ticket but was cool about it. As the years went up on both of us, we would rap from time to time and he helped keep my ear low enough to stay up on the latest street CNN.

He was married and lived in the neighborhood and had two little kids, a first grader and kindergartener. His wife didn't work, she was what Mrs. Brinson called a-house-wife which in this day and age is rare.

A few years ago, Madison got shot in a standoff at the bottom of the Victory Projects. He almost died. Some say it was a set-up, an ambush to be exact. Who knows what the truth is, that story falls right in line with all the mafia tales that float around in our minds about this place we live in.

Madison didn't come off as crooked, if he was you couldn't tell and even if so, I can't condone killing a cop. He spent four months in the ICU with a bullet lodged in the bottom of his lung. Thank God, he made a comeback. The Victory Projects became a blue target after that. Not one speckle of drugs or guns passed through Victory. That was the only time the law-abiding citizens lived over there in peace, but like anything else, time passes and shit goes back to normal and in this city, living under crime was considered normal.

***

Madison sat at the rim of the chair by the window in Browbow's office. I turned the stile and sealed the window shades.

"Now mom and dad, you know that your son has basically confessed to a murder on live television and in front of about a hundred or so people. All who are now first account witnesses to his confession. I can tell you with almost 100% certainty that I think the charge will be involuntary manslaughter. I am not a judge, but I deal with this all the time, and if your son can prove that this was just as he said it was-an accident-then he will be looking at ten months to maybe five years in prison. But if there was a premeditated thought behind this, then…" He shrugged his shoulders high to the bottom of his ears.

"Again, I am not a judge. So before we go any further I need for your son to tell me everything that happened that night from start to finish."

Walter's mother cried more than before. I guess preparing to hear her son's confession twice increased the pain she was feeling and his father just sat in silence not blinking, not moving just sitting quiet as if in a trance.

"Now Walter, tell me again what happened that night," Detective Madison asked. "This time I will be recording you, Officer

Jameson do I have permission to record your son Walter Jameson Junior's version of what happened on the night in question?"

Jameson looked lovingly worried into the face of his wife. She nodded for him to give his consent.

Walter Jr's hands were folded packing one hand rapidly over the other. His mother clutching her chest with her eyes pressed to the ceiling as the tears rolled down onto her lap. Jameson's attention was out the window of Browbows office.

"He was up there alone at the top."

"Who is he Walter? I need you to be specific with this…I need you say his name. Do you understand me; you can start from the part about the other boys and go from there."

Hearing Madison say that to Walter made me understand how hard it was to tell the truth, he, just like me, couldn't say Yosef's name without it causing anguish.

Jameson put his arm around his son. Walter Jr. cleared his throat, wiped his face smearing the tears over his cheeks and continued.

"Yes sir I understand…I wanted to play…not a play here or there, I wanted to be the starting tailback, so my father would be proud of me. I thought about trying to hurt Yosef maybe at practice, hit him in the knee or something but everyone knows on the team not to take low shots at a teammate and Coach woulda been mad at for doing that. I had found out about Marva being pregnant and I knew that Yosef would want to be a good father, then when I was told about the baby not being his that was when I decided to get them dudes involved.

I told Craig Cotton that Yosef wanted to fight him over Marva. At first, he didn't believe me, he said *ain't Yosef your boy*? I said not anymore. I told him that me and Yosef fell out over some money he owed and that we were no longer cool. Craig said if Yosef wanted to fight he was down for it. I told Craig that we always walk home together after our games. It worked out because Rayen played Saturday and we played Friday. I told them how to get to the L and what to do once they got there. I forgot that Isum had that gun on him, so when they saw us coming down the L they stepped out but Yosef wasn't there. I thought Craig would see that and just bounce. Him and the four other dudes started chasing us back up the L. I took off and left Isum by himself.

I ran back up toward the stadium but it was dark and Yosef was gone by then, so I just kept running, that's when I heard a gunshot but it was raining and thundering so hard I wasn't sure. I got home and texted Isum, he never texted me back. I text Yosef next…he didn't text me back either. I sat in my room, looking out the window at the rain, thinking about Isum and if he was okay. This time I called him, it went straight to his voicemail.

I couldn't sleep. I just kept calling and calling Isum's phone. It was 2:30 when Yosef texted me back. I asked him had he heard from Isum, he said no. He said that he was still out, he was sitting on the wheel chair ramp at the library next to the school. He asked me to come up, so I snuck out my backdoor and jogged up to meet up with him.

When I got there, I saw him sitting alone in the corner by the glass doors in the front. He was balled up and shivering cold with his headphones blasting in his ears. I felt sorry for him, he looked so sad, it was the saddest I had ever seen him look. I reached my hand down, he grabbed it and I pulled him up.

I asked him why was he still outside all late. He shrugged his shoulders and started walking down the ramp. The rain had eased off a little. We walked down Ellenwood and cut through a backyard, crossed over Delason until we were back at the stadium. We squeezed through the hole in the fence behind the home stands."

Walter's mouth closed. His eyes looking around the at all the eyes peering back at him. I felt for him and wished I could jump in and save him but there was nothing any us could do but sit, listen and look.

"Do you need to take a break Walter?" Detective Madison asked.

"No sir, I'm good," Walter said.

I felt shame come over me for staring at him like the others. He wasn't a specimen in a glass jar up in Mrs. Browbow's room. He was a kid who was in distress out on a stormy ocean drowning in every word he spoke. I would not stare at him again.

"He walked to the top of the bleachers and sat down. I went and sat with him. He was crying, because when you don't feel wanted…it hurts-it hurts bad. He didn't want to talk, so we just sat there in the rain.

The jealousy I felt toward him had disappeared but then I heard my father's voice in my head again…

Yosef got up and looked over the back of the stadium leaning on the rail. His helmet was next to him on the top bleacher. I picked it up…I picked it up and I hit him over the head. He staggered back, looking at me like a scared kid and that is when he fell off the bleachers."

Walter put his hands over his ears.

"Dad…the sound of his head hitting the bars under the bleachers…I can't get that sound out of my mind…I ran down under there and I tried to see if he was okay, but he wasn't moving. His face…his face was in that muddy water. I ain't never gonna forget his face down in that puddle… never.

I took his helmet and ran. I ran and ran until I got home"

"Why did you take his helmet Walter?" Madison asked.

"I wanted to be him, even if for one night, that is why I took his helmet. He was handsome in his helmet, he looked good in his uniform, spatted up cleats, towel, gloves, he looked like a football player.

I just wanted him to miss a few games so I could play more and show my dad that I was just as good as Yosef was… I just needed a chance to show him that I could play, even if it was for just a couple of games…"

"Walter, how did another helmet end up with the police that night if you took Yosef's?"

"When I got home my helmet was sitting on my bed and I knew that my father would ask me why I have two helmets, so I took mine back up where Yosef was laying…and I sat it next to him and walked away."

"That's when you switched helmets-right?" I said out loud like an impatient little boy.

"Yes Coach," he said.

"I just kept this secret until I spoke with Coach Jones last night and I knew it was time to tell it…it's not fair to Yosef that I did that to him, I took his scholarship."

Walter Jr. collapsed across the table and let out moans of agony that gave off the sound of the dogs of doom. Mrs. Jameson wrapped her arms around him. She was distraught with grief for her son.

Coach Browbow looked at me and I could not speak although my mind was yelling out a million words a minute. I put my head down and looked at the tip of my shoes. Browbow told me to stay in his office until he came back from talking to the student waiting outside.

***

In the far distance, you could hear police sirens racing down the block. Detective Madison handcuffed Walter Jameson Jr. as his father compassionately held his son and walked him out the front door of the school. He leaned over and told his son that he was sorry for everything and that he loved him. Walter's eyes swollen with tears, managed a small smile that was trapped in-between heaven and hell and together, father and son hastily ducked down out of site into the backset of the Police cruiser. The car began to drive slowly through the bus roundabout as the school colors flickered. The cruiser stopped at the end of the school driveway, then turned down Market Street towards downtown drawing fainter and fainter into the distance.

Standing in the schoolhouse door, Big Browbow was holding the box full of Yosef's mementos that I retrieved from the L. He handed it to me. He said that he didn't want that box in his room anymore. I guess he had reached his end with all this and maybe giving me that box would help him take his first step to close this all behind him. I again put it under my right arm and walked out the front door. Hutch was standing under the flagpole. I joined him. I sat the box down on the ground in front of me he reached down and pulled open one side. He rummaged his hands inside and pulled out a worn card that he wrote for Yosef a few weeks ago. He read the words aloud; words that had not washed away down the page. I put my hand on Hutch's shoulder and pulled his head to my thigh and said to him, "this ain't over Hutch, those that endure to the end shall be saved…"

It began to lightly snow and under a gray February sky, the truth was told-of the death of Yosef Nassy #27…

00:00

POST GAME

THE LEARNING

Dusty snow covered the ground. I started my morning off looking out the window at the soft powdery flakes that rested on the bare tree branches. I immediately thought of the coming of spring and what it would bring.

I was slow to get dressed and wanted to call off but I didn't. I exited my house with my coat buttoned up to the bottom of my chin. The wind was shaolin against my face, my eyes watered up from the harshness of the wind. It was winter for sure.

***

It was the next day after Walter got arrested. I hadn't slept all night and probably wouldn't get a good night's sleep for a long time, but that didn't concern me any, but I was tired and afraid of the minutes, days and weeks that laid ahead of me. The facing of my future was real.

I thought about Tim Johnson, the dog in the novel *To Kill a Mockingbird.* Tim Johnson was a mad-dog that was infected with rabies staggering down a dirt road, when Scout and Jem Finch spotted him they ran to get their father.

The first time I read about this dog I didn't see who and what Tim Johnson really symbolized. He represented the infected people of Maycomb County and their racism. Rabies caused Tim Johnson to foam at the mouth, to growl uncontrollably and be aggressive to people that he probably received love from his entire life. The people of that town mouths foamed with the spit of hatred, their growls were growls of anger at a people that they enslaved. I thought hard about that dog and understood the power of what he represented and always thought his name was funny.

Their father and lawyer, Atticus Finch, had to kill Tim Johnson, he had to confront this mad dog that came down the street threatening everyone who lived there, so he took a rifle and shot Tim Johnson dead.

Atticus had to confront the white people of Maycomb as he described them as *"mad dogs that he must confront"* for their treatment and pursuit of a black man named Tom Robinson. Robinson was falsely accused of the rape of a white woman, when in fact it was the other way around. Understand, at the time, white men put white women on a pedestal of sanctity when it came to black men. She was off limits to even look at nevertheless touch, so Tom Robinson had no chance for his life to be saved regardless of anything that Atticus could say or do. The author, Harper Lee killed Tom Robinson in the pages of a book but the real-life Emmett Till was killed five years prior in Money Mississippi basically for the same accusation.

Atticus was successful in killing Tim Johnson but he failed in saving Tom. I guess when I look at it, I failed too. I failed to save Yosef and Isum. I failed to kill the Tim Johnson that hunted them down.

Symbolism is something that I teach in my class. I try and get the students to find the things that may have two meanings to it-like Tim Johnson and racist white folks. The box of mementoes that I had buried in that backroom to the unknowing symbolized the death of a young man, but to me, it was a representation of the pain of this city that cried out into the night. Each object was a link to a different hurt, a different sorrow.

I thought about my future and the things that happened over the past year and how all of these happenings had changed me in many ways, some good and some bad-but changed I was.

My uncles Bible was still in the bottom drawer of my desk getting more brittle each time I picked it up. I gently put it in my hand. I made the decision not to ever open it again, I wanted a new one, and this one would join the rest of my memories and life in the back room of my two-roomed-bungalow.

***

Seasons passed and I decided to pull up my resume on my computer at school. I read over it line by line, each year adding more. My credentials were good and I had enough experience as a teacher and coach to move on to another school district, maybe an all-white one.

They couldn't have all the problems that we have over here at Southside High. If they did, then I know for sure that life ain't never gone show me any slack.

This paper description of my work life could possibly serve as my chance to jump over that fence and start brand new away from this place. And if I did get a real shot to have my own team, I wasn't gonna let a half complete resume blow it for me. I suddenly got excited about what could change my status in a good way.

I made sure to hit the save button and began my search for any potential coaching openings. I was still a newspaper reader for the most part but I was getting good at looking up information on Google and Bing. There were only a few ways to find coaching jobs in the area, one, the paper, by word of mouth or by the internet. I did both.

About two to three weeks after the every season coaching rumors start to fly. This coach is quitting, this coach is getting let go, this coach is moving up to administration. It was usually the being fired that was always on top of the list.

I thought about my years with Coach Browbow. If I decided to leave, would he be happy for me or be the type to deter me from moving up. You would think that I would know him well enough by now to know the answer to that question, but I don't. I tried to put myself in his shoes. How would I feel if my top assistant had the chance to become a head coach? Would I encourage or discourage? Well, I knew myself well enough to say with confidence that I would encourage-no doubt.

I admired Browbow, I admired the way he coached our kids. He was resilient in the worst of times and demanded that we were the same way. He always said that leadership is easy in the good times, when we are winning, but a true leader stands at his best in the rain, snow and times of losing. He was the type of coach that was loved by the majority of his players and despite having many who didn't care for him, to honestly sum him up, he was a players' coach.

He had personality and charm and that was what made the boys want to play for him. He knew the game on both sides of the ball; he was a good example for me to follow and follow him I did.

My uncle had always taught me to attach myself to men that could help me with my goals in my life, but to stay clear of the ones who couldn't. He said those where the niggahs to beware of. That advice sunk deep into my heart and mind so I always did as I was taught.

I spent the next few weeks with my line in the water hoping to catch a bite of a job opening. There was a job at Brownlee Woods High School, a job I know I could never get. The coach got fired for having three losing seasons in a row. Brownlee had a storied past of winning but a few bad seasons was enough to get you gone from a school like that. Southside played them in a basketball game once and we were the only black faces in the building. I don't think they would be ready for me, but I sent my resume to the Athletic Director anyway.

Victory had an opening, but they were just like Southside, actually worse, they barely have a playable field-but off my resume went. Word on the street was the coach quit to take a job in his type of community. That is coded talk for a white coach leaving an all-black school to coach at an all-white school. Some people have a problem with that but I never did. People feel comfortable around there own kind and there ain't no need to force yourself into a bag.

The last opening I found was at a school called Youngstown Heritage. Heritage was a mixed school, it was small, but they played good football. That was the perfect job for me. This job was open due to retirement. I liked this opportunity the best. I was tired of being surround by kids and adults that looked like me. I was in need of a change of pace, face and space. I wasn't superstitious but I kept my fingers crossed over this job.

Three weeks I waited for a phone call, an email, a fax, anything that was a glimmer of hope that I could at least get an interview and get my foot in the door of any of the three. Over my time of waiting patiently, I researched each school, the football and coaching histories, records, playoff appearances and facilities. The one thing about all three that concerned me was that if I did get the job I would be the first black head football coach in the school's history, I at least thought that Victory had to have had a brotha at some point or time running the show, but I was wrong. My uncle used to say that being the first black anything was good and bad, good if you were successful but bad if you are not, because you mess it up for the ones that try to follow your footsteps.

I started my workweek hearing nothing. I decided to wait a few more days before I called only to read in the paper that Brownlee hired a guy from Pittsburg. Some big-time coach with a few state championships under his belt. Now I was down to two. I sorta understood the Brownlee hire, it's hard to turn down a coach with big games on his resume, but I knew that I was qualified for the other two.

The first to finally respond was Victory, the Athletic Director called me and said that he would like to schedule me for an interview. I set it up for next Monday at 3:45. Early Friday morning I got a call from Heritage asking me to come in, I set that one up for Wednesday at 5:30.

I made sure that I was ready, Adrienne asked me questions that we found on google that an AD would ask a potential candidate, questions like; what is your coaching philosophy? What makes you a good candidate? Why should we hire you and how can you make our football program better?

She said I did pretty good with my answers, but in my head, I wasn't so sure, but the real test would be on Monday.

My mind hurried through the day. Southside let out at 2:50 and by 2:55 I was in my car headed to the east side of town. Victory High School was the same as Southside, all black, all poor and mostly broken down but I saw this as a great chance for me because I already knew what they needed but I really wanted the Heritage job.

I rehearsed those questions Adrienne ran by me the other day as I drove. I could feel my nervousness ramping up the closer I got to Victory High. Kids were walking down the street, some with book bags and some without. A group of loud ass rowdy boys their way down the block with a small group of girls laughing behind them. I thought back to my after-school disruptive days walking home talking about all types of inappropriate shit. I wondered if the conversations were the same but probably a little more X-rated.

I pulled up to the school and turned into the parking lot over the mangled blacktop. You could tell from the winter grass that if it were summer, the grass would look the same-half dead. I surveyed the entrance making sure that I was parked in the right spot. Teachers were coming out heading to their respective cars, many looking with the same weary worn out expressions on their faces like we have at Southside after a long day in the battle zone.

I got out and walked to the glass doors. A sawed off security guard opened it up for me before I could reach for the brass handle.

"Afternoon," he said.

"Afternoon," I said back to him.

I walked down the hallway to the office and the secretary instructed me to sit down and wait for the principal to come out and get me. The office had seen better days, the secretary too I thought to myself.

There was a dark skinned boy sitting by himself with his shoulder pressed up against the wooden counter that separated the secretary from anyone who was not supposed to be on her side of the office. His hands hand low between his legs as he rubbed his knuckles back and forth. I sat down next to him. He lifted his head up just enough to cut his eyes to see who I was. I cut my eyes back at him. He quickly dropped his head back down I guess studying the floor or the blood that traced down his fingers. I bumped him with my elbow which rose his head up once again.

"What you do?" I asked him.

He looked at me sideways and mumbled.

"Fightin," he said.

"Where is the other kid, what's his name?"

"He in there with Mr. Greggs, his name is Monroe," he said.

"How many days you get for fighting- this Monroe?' I asked.

"Ten-most of the time, every now then you might catch a five," he said.

"Yeah, ten days is what we give at my school too."

"Youa teacher?"

"Yeah, over at Southside."

"Southside is ass," he said.

I laughed out loud and he smiled.

"You been in with Mr. Greggs yet?" I asked.

"Yeah, I got the ten, jus waiting on my papers."

He looked like he played sports. He reminded of Isum from his build. I figured it wouldn't hurt to ask him if he played football.

"You play football?"

"Yeah, I play fullback and linebacker."

"Cool…what grade are you in?" I asked.

"Tenth."

"You got two years left, but you up here in the office in trouble, what was the fight about?"

"He disrespected my sister."

"What he say," I asked.

"He said she got phat ass."

"Yeah, that is worth fighting for," I said. "But let me ask you this, you ain't gonna fool me into believing that you don't say the same stuff about girls."

"Yeah, but that ain't the same, it's my sister."

"But so are the girls you talk about."

"Monroe plays ball too and we cool, but not when it comes to my sister, sometimes he goes too far," he said.

"Did you explain all this to the Principal?"

"Yeah, that's what I told the Principal the whole story, but he wasn't hearing any of that, you fight you go home 'round here."

"Well…we all have to follow rules in life, might not like all of em but we still gotta follow em," I said.

"I'm Coach Jones, what's your name?"

"I know who you are, I saw you at Yosef's funeral…heard he was a good dude, crazy about his friend killing him though that was wild. My name is Armor Selfhood," he said.

"Armor Selfhood," I repeated with a low drag in my voice.

"My friends call me AS," he said laughing.

"You gon be our new football coach?"

"Hopefully."

"Me too, we need a better coach, the last dude was terrible. He ain't care 'bout us, he bounced on us and took a better job."

"Well, if I get the job Ima need you to not be getting in trouble anymore, understood?"

"I got you Coach, good luck on the job," he said.

"Amor," the secretary called his name.

He got up, grabbed his suspension papers from her and walked out the office door. I couldn't help but think about the rest of the boys on the team and the things I would be facing if I got the job at Victory.

Mr. Greggs came out from his office and shook my hand with who I assumed was Monroe following lazily behind him. I gave Monroe a head nod, he gave one back. Mr. Greggs led me back to a small meeting room. I walked in and was told to sit at the head of the table. The Athletic Director Omar Ibn sat to my right, Mr. Greggs to my left, a parent, a board member and the volleyball coach filled out the remaining chairs around the table.

I had took half of the yellow pill on the sly while I was talking to Amor and I was praying that it kicked in before they dropped question number on me. I could feel my nerves warming up, but I was prepared and ready. I made the decision that I would take the attitude of-*I'm not getting this job anyway and just be myself and do my best.* Greggs fired the first question at me. The others followed in the order from where they sat. Then it was rapid fire from every angle, some that I was prepared for and some that caught me of guard, but I stayed focused on the mission and the goal.

In my head I thought I was doing good but you never really know until it's over and hear some feedback. The last question came from Ibn. He asked me why should I be hired me as the next head coach at Victory High School. I paused and digested the question into my brain. A lifetime of answers and dreams of this chance that confronted me rushed to the shore like soapy ocean water. I sat back in my chair, took a deep breath and sat back up again. I folded my hands in my lap, planted my feet square on the ground underneath me. My eyes circled the faces that had all eyes on me. This was obviously the golden question, the question that seemed to sum up the two hours that I was sitting in this interview.

"You should hire me as your next head coach because I deserve this opportunity. I say this with confidence because I have worked very hard to be in this room being interviewed by you all. I know that I can do this job at a high level, I know this community and the type of talent that comes out of here. I also know the challenges that we all face when it comes to our black boys and the obstacles they deal with every day, the same obstacles that I faced when I was in school. I lost a young man who was very special to me. He had a chance to make it, to make a life for himself. I owe him. I owe this chance that I have-to have the courage to move on, to move forward with my career. I carry him with me in my mind and heart and when I become your new head coach I will give each player on my team the same effort, love and energy that I gave him-then he will be paid back."

Mr. Gregg's eyes quickly scanned the room. I put my head down staring at the laces of my black dress shoes. My thoughts now on Yosef.

"Coach, you did an excellent job and we all thank you for your time and what you do for our young men. Either way Coach you will be hearing from me. Our interview process wraps up Friday and we are hoping to have a decision no later than next Tuesday-Wednesday at the latest. I hope that timetable can work for you," Mr. Greggs said.

"Yes it does," I said. "Mr. Greggs, can I ask you a question?"

"Yes."

"That kid that was behind you when I was coming in, was that the infamous Monroe?"

"Coach, you got a good eye, yes that was Monroe Early, best player on the team but man he loves to clown more than anything. He has all-state talent but only gives an all-nothing effort, it's frustrating to watch him play to be honest."

I walked out into the evening air with my mind on two things, Yosef and what to eat but I did feel the relief of having one interview under my belt. This experience definitely made me ready for the heritage interview because that was the job I really wanted anyway.

***

I pulled up into the Heritage parking lot that was surrounded by flower beds waiting to bloom anticipating the coming of spring. Three students waited in the lobby, two boys and a girl. All three were dressed nicely. They walked up to me and welcomed me to heritage

High School. This was their job I guessed, to escort coaching candidates to the waiting area, a big difference from the no greeting I got at Victory. The young lady handed me a bottle of water and pointed to where the restrooms where located. So far, it was a class act operation.

I was called back to the brightly lit room. Pictures adorned the walls of old buildings and new construction that took place a few years ago. I was placed in the center of the long meeting table that was flanked by the people who would be conducting the interview.

I pulled out my handouts that would give intricate details of my dream football program. I had had spent weeks perfecting the typed information that was in in there.

Questions came rapidly as my answers were being scored for thoroughness and believability. The interview lasted two hours.

The Heritage interview went smoothly as planned and hey informed me that a decision would be made in a couple of days. The Principal Eric Tropinin thanked me for coming and walked me to my car.

"Coach Jones, you did an excellent job in there, if it was up to me, I would offer you the job today, but we have to finish up a few more interviews. You made a good impression on me at least, either way good luck to you."

"Thank you, and I appreciate you bringing me in for an interview."

"Coach before you go, question-are you interviewing anyplace else?" he asked me.

"Yes, I interviewed at Victory High School on Monday."

"Victory?" he said with a smirk on his face.

"Yes."

"How did that go, I'm sure they offered you that job on the spot."

"No, they told me pretty much what you did that it would be a few days before I hear a yes or no."

"That's a tough job over there, I would think that you would want to get away from a coaching job like that one, but they do have good people over there. It's just hard to consistently win at schools like

Southside. But you guys did a great job over there, so maybe I'm wrong."

"Yeah, Coach Browbow has the program rolling pretty good."

"Well anyway Coach, again thank you and we will be in touch."

I rode away replaying the interview in my head and questioning if I did my best despite what the principal said. Heritage is the best job for me no doubt and if they offer it to me, I am going to take it.

I went home at ease because my interviews were over and now the waiting game begins. That evening I got a call from Mr. Tropinin at Heritage.

"Coach Jones…this is Principal Tropinin from Heritage High School…How are you this evening?"

"I'm good, how about you?"

"I'm good as well, Coach, I am calling on behalf of the Heritage Athletic Department, Board of Education and myself, we would like to offer you the head football coaching position pending on board approval should you accept.

Coach, you do not have to say yes or no tonight, I know you just interviewed today but you impressed us all so much that we decided as a team to pull the trigger and offer you the job. However Coach, this a time sensitive situation, we have a second candidate in place that we will offer this too if you decline and out of courtesy, we don't want him waiting in limbo longer than needed.

When do you think you can have an answer for me Coach? In the meantime I would like to bring you back tomorrow and take you on a short tour of our facilities, can you stop up about 4:00?"

I was smiling and if a smile made a sound, it would be as loud as the sirens I hear at night around my house.

"Sure I can and thank you, this means a lot and I can have my answer for you by Friday if that is okay?"

"Great, I will see you tomorrow sir."

I immediately called Adrienne and told her my good news. She asked if I had heard anything form Victory, I hadn't. I told her that was going to take the Heritage job after the tour tomorrow. My mind was made up already but I wasn't going to act thirsty and call Tropinin back and tell him until that tour was over.

My drive home, the people, the places all seemed clean and new. I was happy and proud of myself. I pulled in my driveway not noticing the uneven pavement that my wheels rolled over every day.

That night in my room, I looked out the window watching the snow land on top of the parked cars on the street. It was late, but I couldn't sleep because I was excited about the morning coming and eventually the afternoon.

I took my car keys off the night table and walked to the back of the house to the door of the room that I had locked away my past. I palmed the key and nudged it up to my fingers, I unlocked the dead-bolt and fought my way through the smell of old papers and the poor ventilation. I grabbed the shoe box off the shelf that was full of pictures, articles of old football games, receipts and a bunch of other shit.

I rummaged through the box of Yosef's death and I could still feel the emotion and pain of his memory that was permanent in my mind. He was not lost to the world, his life was in this box, written on a card, in the fabric of a teddy bear, in the metal of the door key.

I came in here because change had come for me in the form of opportunity to start new and fresh and I wanted to share it with my Uncle and Yosef. I laid down in my old bed, hearing the creaks and squeaks from the wear of all the years. I folded my arms behind my head and stared at the ceiling.

Monroe Early and Armor Selfhood came to my vision like a hologram or a ghost. *Armor looks like Isum to me* I thought.

He was a nice kid…who took a suspension to protect his sister… that is something I would have done too…Armor Selfhood, an honorable young man and Monroe Early the young man who tested that honor.

I fell asleep with my clothes on.

Lay this Laurel on the One
Too intrinsic for Renown-
Laurel-veil your deathless tree-
Him you chasten-that is He!

-Emily Dickinson, 1393

ABOUT THE AUTHOR

Devlin was born and raised in the valley of Youngstown, Ohio. His mind was fashioned from the same steel that was produced in the small city that boarders the state of Pennsylvania. Devlin is an Artist, Author, Hip-Hop Historian & Movie Critic (the first two being his real occupations). His artistic and writing style is unique all to its own however; you can clearly see and read his influences. The influences of Artist Ernie Barnes, Charles White, Arron Douglas, Jacob Lawrence, the writings of Walter Mosely, Richard Wright, Alfred Hitchcock, Robert Beck, August Wilson, Attica Locke, Chester Himes, Danny Gardner, Donald Goines & of course, Luke Cage, Black Panther, the Hulk and Iron Fist in the world of comic books.

He became a fan of movies while sitting as a child with his Grandfather Thomas 'Doc' Smith, who loved classic black films and mystery noir along with the 1940's gangster genre, with stars like James Cagney, Sidney Poitier, James Stewart, Claudia McNeil, Brock Peters, Ossie Davis, Spencer Tracy, Ruby Dee, James Edwards, Humphrey Bogart, Melvin Van Peebles, Harry Belafonte, Henry Fonda, Jane Fonda, Lauren Bacall, Lena Horne, Ivan Dixon, Robert Mitchum, Ida Lupino, John Garfield and Basil Rathbone. Those movies created a passion for film and the big screen experience. Add those names in with movies like To Kill a Mockingbird, Jaws, Sherlock Holmes, In the Heat of the Night, The Outsiders, How Green Was My Valley, A Soldier's Story, The Learning Tree, Anthony Loves Angela and many more.

It was sports, in particular football that carried Devlin to college where he studied Illustration, Reading & Art Education and after graduation, he took on the life of a teacher, artist, writer and football coach.

Devlin lives in his own world full of unpainted canvases and untold stories based out of his own experiences. He travels through the pages of the stories he writes similar to the ink that flows from a pen. He goes by many names and titles, all feeding into the characters that appear through his work; Antietam Jones, Duff Anderson, Carl Lucas, John Kane, Pickle, DC, The 5th Scientific Supreme, Awkh5, John Stewart, Earth 515, and his favorite Bumble Bee (killa-bee).

He makes art for the people.

{An-tee-tuh-m}

www.ingramcontent.com/pod-product-compliance
Lightning Source LLC
Chambersburg PA
CBHW031535260326
41914CB00032B/1819/J

9781953975904